From Forgiven
to Faithfulness

From Forgiven to Faithfulness
2 Timothy, Titus, Philemon

This inductive Bible study is designed for individual, small group, or classroom use. A leader's guide with full lesson plans and the answers to the Bible study questions is available from Regular Baptist Press. Order RBP0001 online at www.regularbaptistpress.org, e-mail orders@rbpstore.org, call toll-free 1-800-727-4440, or contact your distributor.

REGULAR BAPTIST PRESS
1300 North Meacham Road
Schaumburg, Illinois 60173-4806

The Doctrinal Basis of Our Curriculum

A more detailed statement with references is available upon request.

- The verbal, plenary inspiration of the Scriptures
- Only one true God
- The Trinity of the Godhead
- The Holy Spirit and His ministry
- The personality of Satan
- The Genesis account of creation
- Original sin and the fall of man
- The virgin birth of Christ
- Salvation through faith in the shed blood of Christ
- The bodily resurrection and priesthood of Christ
- Grace and the new birth
- Justification by faith
- Sanctification of the believer

- The security of the believer
- The church
- The ordinances of the local church: baptism by immersion and the Lord's Supper
- Biblical separation— ecclesiastical and personal
- Obedience to civil government
- The place of Israel
- The pretribulation rapture of the church
- The premillennial return of Christ
- The millennial reign of Christ
- Eternal glory in Heaven for the righteous
- Eternal torment in Hell for the wicked

FROM FORGIVEN TO FAITHFULNESS: 2 TIMOTHY, TITUS, PHILEMON
Adult Bible Study Book
Vol. 57, No. 3
© 2009
Regular Baptist Press • Schaumburg, Illinois
www.regularbaptistpress.org • 1-800-727-4440
Printed in U.S.A.
All rights reserved
RBP0004 • ISBN: 978-1-59402-923-3

Contents

Preface

The wonder of a caterpillar changing into a butterfly is forever amazing. Perhaps no transformation in God's creation is as radical and beautiful. However, in the spiritual realm, the transformation of a sinner into a faithful servant of God is just as radical and beautiful.

Philemon, Titus, and 2 Timothy focus upon *forgiveness, righteousness, and faithfulness.* We enter upon the Christian life as God grants us forgiveness in Jesus Christ. As we grow in Christ, our lives become increasingly characterized by righteousness. And God expects faithfulness from us, His servants, until He takes us home to be with Him.

Philemon serves to illustrate how God forgives humans overtaken by an unpayable debt of sin. Titus presents righteous standards of living for God's children and leaders. And 2 Timothy stresses the importance of faithfulness to God in all areas of life.

This study presents these three epistles in the reverse of their order in the Bible for two reasons. First of all, this order will be the order in which Paul wrote them, and the chronological sequence will aid in understanding. Second, this order will provide a logical sequence for the themes of forgiveness, righteousness, and faithfulness. You should feel the value and need of these qualities and make personal strides in developing them in your life.

A Story of Forgiveness

The forgiveness God has extended to us
serves as the reason and the measure
for our forgiving others.

Philemon

"And be ye kind one to another, tenderhearted, forgiving one another, even as God for Christ's sake hath forgiven you" (Ephesians 4:32).

Sometimes the simplest tasks can become complicated. For instance, a young man decided to make macaroni and cheese. He read the directions on the box and poured the noodles into the boiling water when he noticed that there didn't seem to be enough noodles for even one person. So he poured in another box of macaroni noodles. But that still didn't seem like enough for his appetite. He then added a third box of noodles. Finally the pot looked full enough to satisfy his hunger.

Ten minutes later the young man realized that Kraft did know what they were doing when they packaged their macaroni noodles. He had so much macaroni that he could have eaten it for the next week. His simple task had turned into a fiasco.

Asking forgiveness seems like a simple task, but when we go to do it, we can turn it into something that is more than we can handle.

This study focuses on Paul's appeal for forgiveness on behalf of his new brother in Christ.

Getting Started

1. Why is granting forgiveness difficult sometimes?

2. What might make granting forgiveness easier?

Searching the Scriptures

Prison Letter

Paul began his letter calling himself a "prisoner of Jesus Christ" because he wrote while under house arrest in Rome, awaiting his hearing before Caesar. His incarceration had resulted from preaching the gospel of Christ and not from breaking human laws.

3. Read Philemon 1. How does Paul calling himself a prisoner instead of an apostle set up the tone of his letter?

4. Why would the tone of Paul's letter be important?

Timothy, a young man from the area of Derbe and Lystra, had joined Paul on Paul's second missionary journey (Acts 16:1–3). He served faithfully, both as a companion and as a messenger of Paul until the end of Paul's life.

Paul addressed this letter to Philemon, a man whom he loved as a brother in the family of God and a fellow in the service of Jesus Christ. Paul further mentioned Apphia and Archippus as addressees of his letter. Apphia probably was the wife of Philemon, and Archippus, the son of Philemon and Apphia.

Paul encouraged Archippus to fulfill the ministry he had received in the Lord (Colossians 4:17). Archippus may have served as pastor of the church that met in Philemon's home (Philemon 2).

Paul designated him a fellow soldier (v. 2), for Paul saw Archippus fighting the same spiritual enemies that he was fighting. Certainly these enemies included the evil spirit powers (Ephesians 6:11, 12).

5. What similarities exist between the spiritual battles of Paul's day and our day?

Dear Church

It is significant that Paul included the church as an intended recipient of this letter (Philemon 2). The letter urged Philemon to forgive his runaway slave, Onesimus, who had become a believer. It also informed the church to receive Onesimus and offer him all the blessings of church fellowship. If the church met in Philemon's house and was to receive Onesimus as an active member, then Philemon should publicly receive Onesimus with full forgiveness.

6. Read Colossians 1:12–14. What do these verses say about the cost to God the Father and God the Son of providing forgiveness for us?

Although Paul was restricted as a prisoner, he maintained a constant prayer life, mentioning Christians throughout the world by name and commending them to the grace of God.

Prayers of Thanks

Paul was thankful for Philemon because he had heard good reports about him. Possibly Epaphras, who was with Paul in Rome (Philemon 23) and who had taken news from Colosse to Paul had told Paul about Philemon. These "beloved brothers" in the Lord eagerly desired to share with one another the events of their lives and service for Christ. Having no phones or e-mail and little mail, personal messengers shuttled from church to the apostle and back bearing tidings.

The reports told Paul of Philemon's "love and faith . . . toward the Lord Jesus, and toward all saints" (v. 5). Philemon had faith toward the Lord Jesus and love toward all the saints. "Saints" in the Bible are all those set apart by faith in Christ, not a special class of super-Christians and certainly not merely dead Christians. Paul specified "all saints," meaning all those with whom Philemon came into contact.

7. How would faith and love play vital roles in Philemon's forgiveness of Onesimus, or in any believer's forgiveness of another believer?

Philemon had shown love to all the saints, and Paul wrote, hoping that Philemon would include Onesimus as an object of his love.

8. Record a situation you have faced where faith and love were key in handling the matter.

Prayers of Request

In verses 6 and 7, Paul explained the request he was making to God on behalf of Philemon. Paul's thought in verse 6 is that Philemon's faith in God had led him to accept the needy and to be generous toward them. It would be a tragedy if those who received his fellowship perceived it as mere human kindness. Therefore, Paul prayed that people might come to acknowledge that the character qualities, "every good thing," which moved Philemon to generosity were from Christ. Then they would give glory unto Him. Paul prayed that Philemon's practical love would bring glory to Christ.

9. How will those to whom we show love and kindness discern that Christ deserves the glory for our actions toward them?

Paul possessed the authority of an apostle of Jesus Christ. He could have simply ordered Philemon to receive Onesimus and warned him of the consequences of disobedience. However, Paul chose to appeal to him instead.

10. Read Philemon 8 and 9. What do you think Philemon would be thinking as he reached this point in the letter?

Love Appeal

Paul appealed to Philemon on the basis of love. This love could have been Philemon's love for Paul and Timothy specifically, or his love for believers in general. Ultimately, of course, Philemon's love was the love of God working through him as a believer (Galatians 5:22).

11. Read Philemon 9. How would Paul's mention of his imprisonment impact Philemon?

Cautiously and tactfully, Paul laid the groundwork for asking Philemon to receive back his runaway slave. However, to this point Paul had not mentioned Onesimus by name, or even the specific request for which he was writing. Certainly, Philemon would have been intrigued when he read Paul's words in verses 8 and 9.

"Useful"

Paul delayed using Onesimus' name as long as possible, finally mentioning it a third of the way through his letter. Only after calling him "my son" and again recalling the prison situation in which he had begotten Onesimus does he name the runaway slave.

Before Onesimus was saved ("in time past") he was "unprofitable" (Philemon 11). His service in Philemon's household may have been average or even better, but the quality of his service was overshadowed by his colossal failure in running away.

Now that Onesimus had been saved, he was profitable to both Paul and Philemon. Interestingly, Onesimus' name means "useful." He failed to live up to that name before he became a Christian, but as a Christian he was truly "Onesimus," the useful, profitable one.

Onesimus probably had been serving Paul since the time of his conversion and would have been a great help if Paul had retained him in Rome. He may have reported to Paul the evidences of Philemon's faith and love that he had seen while an unsaved slave in the household.

12. Read Philemon 11. How could Onesimus become useful to Philemon?

The culture of that day believed that a slave was his master's property. Paul, in the spirit of 1 Corinthians 7:21–23, returned Philemon's property. However, the tender affection of Paul for his son in the faith is evident. As Onesimus came to Colosse, it was as though Paul's own heart traveled with him.

In Your Stead

Paul wanted Philemon to know that sending Onesimus back was not a simple decision. Because Paul was very limited due to his house arrest, Onesimus could have served him in many helpful ways. Paul described this potential ministry, not as bond service to which the servant is obligated, but as a service that is beneficial to the one served.

Suppose Paul had kept Onesimus as a servant to himself. Then Paul would have considered Onesimus as serving "in thy [Philemon's] stead" (Philemon 13), since the runaway belonged to Philemon.

13. Read Philemon 13. What great salvation truth is illustrated by "in thy stead" in this situation?

If Onesimus had stayed in Rome serving Paul, his service would have been at Philemon's expense ("thy benefit," v. 14) because Philemon would have lost the service of Onesimus in his own household. Paul would not keep the slave without consultation with and the approval of Philemon. Paul knew if he were to keep Onesimus without first discussing the matter with Philemon, it might appear that Philemon was unwilling. Paul decided to avoid all appearance of coercion (vv. 15, 16).

Onesimus had "departed [only] for a season," for he was returning (v. 15) —and what a glorious return it was. He returned as a brother in Christ to both Paul and Philemon (v. 16). Philemon should be smitten with a double love for Onesimus—"in the flesh, and in the Lord."

Paul thought that perhaps God had allowed Onesimus to run away in order to bring him to Himself. Therefore, Paul spoke of the flight in the passive voice as though Onesimus had fulfilled God's plan in leaving (Philemon 15). Of course, Onesimus would still have been accountable to God for committing such a sinful deed. Since God had not given Paul a special revelation concerning Onesimus' flight, Paul was not dogmatic. He said that "perhaps" Onesimus departed through the purpose of God.

14. How should Paul's "perhaps" affect Philemon's decision to forgive Onesimus?

Surely God was returning the slave, and Philemon should receive him (v. 15). The word "receive" can be used of receiving a payment. Onesimus' return was God's payment to Philemon for his faithfulness to the Lord through the whole difficult affair.

At the Heart

In verse 17, Paul boldly asked Philemon to receive Onesimus. If Philemon considered Paul his partner in Christ, he should receive Onesimus as though he were Paul himself.

Paul also took responsibility for his spiritual son's debts. Paul wrote the promise of payment in his own hand, which would make it binding according to Roman law. However, the indirectness of Paul's statement about the debt gave Philemon the opportunity to spare Paul from paying.

Before Philemon decided to accept Paul's offer of payment, he should remember two things. First, in some way he, too, was saved as a result of Paul's ministry (v. 19). Second, Paul had just done him a great service by returning his runaway slave as a beloved brother.

15. Read Philemon 20. How could Philemon give Paul great joy and refreshment?

Paul was confident that Philemon would heed his appeal and so obey God (v. 21). In fact, Paul expected him to do even more than receive Onesimus. This "more" could include dismissing the debt without charging it to Paul and granting Onesimus his freedom from slavery.

As Paul brought the letter to a close, he addressed his personal future. He expressed trust that he would be released from bondage in answer to prayer (v. 22). He anticipated a visit to Colosse and even to Philemon's home. Perhaps the very mention of a possible visit by Paul was a gentle nudge to Philemon to do as Paul had asked.

The prayers for Paul's deliverance were not merely the prayers of Philemon but of the believers as a group. Therefore, the letter ends with a reminder that the entire church, not only one man, was in Paul's mind as he wrote. Philemon was on the spot before all the church to walk in the way of righteousness with regard to Onesimus.

Making It Personal

16. Do you need to extend forgiveness to someone?

17. What specific steps should you take?

18. When will you take the first step?

19. Memorize Ephesians 4:32.

Forgiven!

*God's amazing forgiveness is to permeate
our thoughts, be proclaimed to others,
and practiced.*

Matthew 18:21–35; Luke 7:36–50; 17:3–5; 23:34; Acts 7:51–60

"In whom we have redemption through his blood, the forgiveness of sins, according to the riches of his grace" (Ephesians 1:7).

Husbands are notorious for being insensitive. They say things like, "You aren't going to wear that are you?" And, "Is this supposed to taste this bland?" Or, "Are you going to put some makeup on today?"

Needless to say, husbands who say such insensitive things have developed a long list of ways to say they're sorry. Buying flowers and going out for dinner are a couple of the more popular ones.

Sometimes a wife will corner her husband and ask him for his honest opinion about how she looks. In those cases, the husband should press the speed dial button for the local florist before he even answers his wife. If his wife wants an opinion, then she has already come to the conclusion that she doesn't like her shoes, dress, or hairstyle that is in question. The husband is hopelessly doomed. He can either tell the truth or lie. Either way, his wife won't be happy with his answer.

Getting Started

1. Why do we often feel that a person's verbal request for forgiveness is not enough to make up for what the person did to us?

2. What would happen if God felt that way toward us?

Searching the Scriptures

This study will go into detail on God's kind of forgiveness. You will come to appreciate it more and to model your own forgiveness after it.

Paul's letter to Philemon addressed the personal problems of a runaway slave and his master. Paul provided guidance based on the wisdom of God, not mere human wisdom. Therefore, the firm foundation of Christian theology underlies the prescriptions of Philemon. Some of the prescriptions Paul gave Philemon for dealing with his rebellious servant parallel the way God deals with His rebellious humans when they return to Him. So, it should not be surprising that Philemon was to deal with his disobedient servant like God deals with disobedient people.

3. Read 1 John 2:6. How should the believer's walk on this earth compare with Christ's walk?

The book of Philemon illustrates the basic Christian truth of forgiveness. The common Greek words for forgiveness in the Bible mean "to let go," "to release," "to pardon," or "to forgive." They were used in the secular Greek language to speak of letting go a debt, of releasing a prisoner, or of canceling criminal proceedings. However, when these words speak of God's forgiveness of a sinner, they are lifted to unparalleled heights of meaning.

The Background for Forgiveness

The dark velvet cloth of the jeweler makes his gems appear to glisten most brightly. In a similar manner, the enormity of sin makes God's forgiveness shine with splendor. An understanding of God's estimate of the lost produces deep appreciation of His gracious work to forgive.

The natural tendency of the sinful human heart is to compare ourselves to one another, especially to another who happens to fall slightly behind us at the point of comparison.

4. Read 1 Peter 1:15. By what standard does God measure us?

God sees that "all have sinned, and come short of the glory of God" (Romans 3:23). We possess an evil heart (Mark 7:21–23) and are full of unrighteousness (Romans 1:28–32).

5. Read Romans 1:28. What does this verse mention as an underlying problem with sinful people?

God warns that we are deceived by our own hearts (Jeremiah 17:9). We, like wandering sheep, are lost and unable to find our way to God (Luke 19:10). We stand condemned before the Judge of the universe, and His wrath abides on us, just waiting to be poured out against us (John 3:18, 36).

6. What illustrations would you use to describe the sinful state of man?

Forgiveness enters the ominous picture of man's sinfulness. God's forgiveness releases us from the death penalty of sin. Only God could forgive us because our offenses have been against Him (Psalm 51:4).

7. Read Micah 7:18 and 19. What two words would you use to describe God's forgiveness of sins?

The Basis of Forgiveness

How can a just and righteous God forgive sin? He can forgive humans only because God the Son has paid the penalty in our place. Forgiveness is found only in Christ, Who provided it through His death.

When Christ shed His blood at Calvary, He bore our sins in His own body on the Cross (1 Peter 2:24). He suffered the death penalty of sin so that the Father could forgive us that penalty. By His grace God forgives those who put their faith in Christ.

8. What illustrations would you use to describe the richness of God's grace?

God provided an accurate foreshadowing of the bloody death of Christ in the animal sacrifices of the Old Testament. Those sacrifices spoke as great object lessons, telling the world of the Lamb of God Who would come to take away the sins of the world. They also proclaimed that forgiveness could come from God only by the shedding of blood (Hebrews 9:22).

God established that shed blood was the foundation of forgiveness as far back as the fall of Adam and the coverings of animal skins He made for Adam and Eve. When Christ offered the perfect sacrifice, full forgiveness was provided and there was no further need for animal sacrifices (Hebrews 10:18).

First John 4:10 describes Christ's death as the propitiation for our sins. "Propitiation" means to appease or atone. God's holiness was satisfied and His wrath appeased. Therefore, God could remain just and at the same time justify, or declare righteous, the ungodly (Romans 3:26).

God's forgiveness applies to all our sins, for He tells us that those in Christ are under no condemning judgment whatsoever (Romans 8:1).

9. How do you show that you value forgiveness of sins in your life?

Forgiveness Reminders

The ordinances God has given to the church continually remind Christians of God's forgiveness.

Baptism speaks of forgiveness, according to Acts 2:38. It reads, "Then Peter said unto them, Repent, and be baptized every one of you in the name of Jesus Christ for the remission of sins." The word "for" in this verse means "because of" or "on the basis of." Peter was commanding those who had heard the gospel to be baptized as an expression of the repentance and forgiveness that they had already experienced. Thus, water baptism follows forgiveness—salvation—and is a public reminder of this great salvation truth.

10. What do you think about when you witness a baptism? Do you consciously remember God's forgiveness of sins?

The Lord's Supper also speaks of forgiveness. The night before His death, Christ instituted the Lord's Supper observance. He explained the symbolism of the cup with these words: "For this is my blood of the new testament, which is shed for many for the remission [forgiveness] of sins" (Matthew 26:28). The periodic communion service should remind everyone present that God graciously forgives sin on the basis of Christ's shed blood.

11. What do you tend to think about at a Communion service? Do you consciously remember God's forgiveness of sins when you take part in the Lord's Supper?

Forgiveness Proclaimed

Those forgiven by God are to proclaim His forgiveness to others. Luke's account of the Great Commission records Christ's great statement of purpose (Luke 24:47, 48).

12. Read Luke 24:47 and 48. How seriously should we take Jesus' commission?

Paul confessed that God commanded us to preach Christ as the Judge of all men and "that through his name whosoever believeth in him shall receive remission [forgiveness] of sins" (Acts 10:42, 43). Paul obeyed that command (13:38, 39).

13. How will we know whether we take Jesus' commission to us seriously?

Practicing Forgiveness

The Lord Jesus Christ prayed from the cross, "Father, forgive them; for they know not what they do" (Luke 23:34). He was asking forgiveness for those who were in the process of putting Him to death.

14. Read Luke 23:24. What else, if anything, could Jesus have said from the cross that would have better communicated His loving, forgiving heart?

The apostle Peter wrote inspired words to some suffering children of God. He told them to follow the example of Christ, "who, when he was reviled, reviled not again; when he suffered, he threatened not; but committed himself to him that judgeth righteously" (1 Peter 2:23). On the cross, Christ did not return evil for evil.

The Lord has left us an example that we should follow in His steps. Surely, it is inconceivable that we would consider offenses against us as more serious, and thus less forgivable, than the offenses committed against Christ. Believers, like Christ, should be known as forgiving people.

15. Acts 7:59 and 60. In what ways did Stephen follow Christ's example?

Forgive!

Believers follow the command of God, as well as the pattern of Christ, in forgiving others. Peter once asked the Lord how many times he must forgive a brother who sinned against him. He offered to forgive seven times. Jesus replied that seven times would not be adequate, and He set the requirement at 70 times 7, or 490 times (Matthew 18:21, 22). In other words, the Lord said believers must not limit their forgiveness to a calculated number of times.

16. Read Ephesians 4:32. Do you think you could ever fully live this verse out? Why or why not?

God commands believers to forgive like He forgave them. And like the servant of the king in Christ's story, believers have been forgiven much by God. What people do to believers here on earth is relatively insignificant, compared with what the believer has done to violate God's holiness. If He can forgive the saint, then the saint should be able to forgive others.

Monopoly on Revenge

When one fails to forgive, he or she harbors an unforgiving spirit and seeks revenge, either actively or passively by waiting and hoping that it happens. God warns about revenge in Romans 12:19. God holds a monopoly on vengeance. But, how can one overcome the strong urges of the flesh to get even?

When Christ was on earth, He summed up the entire law of God, which expressed God's holiness, in the commandments to love God and to love our neighbor. Our love for our neighbor should be as great as our love for ourselves. This love shows itself as caring concern. Forgiveness will spring from a heart that really cares about the other person (1 Corinthians 13:4–8). If we genuinely want what is best for another, we will not harbor an unforgiving spirit or seek revenge. We will deal with our feelings and do what would enhance the eternal welfare of the other person.

17. Evaluate this statement: I will forgive that person when I feel like forgiving that person.

The Lord told His disciples that if their brother should trespass against them and repent, they should forgive him. And even if he should trespass and repent seven times in one day, they should forgive him. The disciples' response was, "Lord, increase our faith" (Luke 17:5). The disciples realized such forgiveness is not natural. One must have faith to believe that it is God's will, or he will never call upon the Lord in faith to help him forgive. One must have faith that God will take care of the offender, or he will seek revenge and not give place to the wrath of God.

It is a great blessing to be forgiven by God. It is also a great blessing to be forgiven by others and to be forgiving of others.

Making It Personal

18. How would you describe God's forgiveness?

19. What could you do to remember His forgiveness on a regular basis?

20. With whom should you share the message of God's forgiveness?

21. Memorize Ephesians 1:7.

Godly Leadership

God has requirements for godly leadership.

Titus 1

"For this cause left I thee in Crete, that thou shouldest set in order the things that are wanting, and ordain elders in every city, as I had appointed thee" (Titus 1:5).

Schools are realizing what believers have known for years: character counts. Knowledge is a wonderful tool, but character puts knowledge to use. For example, a math whiz with bad character may grow up to cheat employees out of their retirement accounts while he pays himself millions of dollars. A math whiz with good character may grow up to save his company money and increase the salaries of her fellow employees.

The Lord requires godly character of leaders in His church. This study focuses on God's requirements for godly leadership.

Getting Started

1. How important is character?

2. Why do you rate its importance as you do?

Searching the Scriptures

After opening greetings, Paul's letter immediately turned to emphasizing the godly qualities church leaders must possess. Paul also demonstrated why godly leadership was so important to the churches of Crete (Titus 1:10–16).

Greetings

Paul did not think of himself more highly than he ought, for he saw himself as a bondservant of God (Titus 1:1). A bondservant was a slave who had willingly surrendered his freedom to spend himself serving another.

3. Read Titus 1:1. Why would you expect a "servant of God" to be a godly leader?

In the same breath Paul called himself an apostle of Jesus Christ. The apostles of Christ were a select few. They had seen the Lord, been chosen by the Lord, been commissioned by Him to proclaim God's Word, and had miracle-working power from God. An apostle was also a person of honor and authority. Paul wrote as the humble bondservant with great authority from God.

Paul's life and message measured up to a standard—the faith shared by God's elect and the truth, which produces godly living (v. 1). Paul's beliefs were orthodox and his lifestyle was godly.

Paul's life and message also had a fixed foundation, being grounded upon the hope of eternal life. Paul referred to his future salvation from the presence of sin when he wrote of the "hope of eternal life" (v. 2). Any hope based on the promise of God is a sure hope.

4. Read Titus 1:4. Since Titus was one of Paul's converts to Christ, how would you expect Titus to view godly living?

Titus, the recipient of Paul's letter (v. 4), may have come from Antioch in Syria, for Paul took him from there to Jerusalem as an example that a saved Gentile was not required to be circumcised (Acts 15:2; Galatians 2:1–3).

Paul had been in prison when he wrote to Philemon, and he anticipated being released. Apparently he was released, and in his travels he proclaimed the gospel on the island of Crete. However, the new converts were not yet established into organized local churches when Paul departed. Paul left Titus in Crete to complete the founding of the churches and to ordain godly leaders in those churches.

5. Read Titus 1:5. How successful do you think a weak spiritual leader would have been at the tasks that Paul gave to Titus?

This letter to Titus offered Paul's encouragement and instruction for this demanding task. Paul's theme, as mentioned, was godliness. If the churches of Crete were to be godly, then they must have godly leaders.

6. Why would the same be true of our churches today?

Paul mentions "elders" (v. 5) and a "bishop" (v. 7) in his discussion of leadership. Notice that both titles are used of the same office. Titus was to ordain elders. The list of qualifications for such elders begins in verse 6 and continues in verses 7–9 with the introductory statement that "a bishop must be." The flow of thought indicates that the elder is the bishop.

Feed the Flock

Peter wrote that elders are to "feed the flock of God," and if they do well they will be rewarded by the Chief Shepherd of that flock, Jesus Christ (1 Peter 5:1–4). The word "feed" is simply a verb form of "shepherd" or "pastor," and could properly be translated "pastor the flock of God" (v. 2). So, the elder or bishop is to pastor the church.

The term "pastor" or "shepherd" emphasizes that the leader feeds and cares for God's people. The term "elder" or "older" emphasizes that the leader is mature and sets an example for God's people. And the term "bishop" or "overseer" emphasizes that the leader guides and directs God's people.

Note that the qualifications for a bishop are spiritual qualifications. God requires, and a church needs, godly men for leadership. Obviously, no man will be perfect in all these qualities, or even in any of them. But every pastor must show a recognizable level of maturity in these things, and he should be making progress continually in them.

"Blameless" (v. 6) refers to a reputation among the people of God that there are no charges of wrongdoing against him.

7. Read 1 Timothy 3:10. Why is it important for a deacon to also exhibit blamelessness? Doesn't a deacon deal more with the church's money and building than he does with the spiritual well-being of church members?

A steward is one who manages the things of another (Titus 1:7). A pastor's blamelessness in personal stewardship indicates the ability to function blamelessly in shepherding others.

A One-Woman Man

The pastor must also be the husband of one wife (v. 6). God said one man should marry one woman, and that relationship should continue until broken by death (Matthew 19:3–12).

8. Read Ephesians 5:25 and 1 Peter 3:7. What instruction for godly husbands is found in these verses?

The pastor must set the example, being a one-woman man who gives his heart completely to his wife.

The pastor must also have faithful children.

9. Read 1 Timothy 3:4 and 5. Why must a pastor be able to rule his own household well?

Leading a home is similar to leading a church. Both are composed of people needing love, instruction in living, correction, and orderly functioning. A man's failure to lead his own home to faith in Christ would indicate a weakness in leadership.

"Not self-willed" (v. 7) means to please one's self. The pastor must avoid hedonism. Rather, the pastor ministers for the glory of God, for the edification of saints, and for the salvation of the lost.

Unresolved anger seething within may erupt in a steaming stream of anger, over seemingly little irritations. Such a person is "soon angry" (v. 7). The godly pastor treats his flock gently (1 Timothy 3:3).

Not alongside Wine

"Not given to wine" (v. 7) is the next requirement for pastors. Wine in Bible times was either nonalcoholic fresh juice or fermented juice. Even the fermented variety usually had an alcoholic content far below 14 percent, and it was almost always diluted with water before being consumed. In other words, even alcoholic wine, as commonly drunk, was so weak in alcoholic content that a large volume of it would need to be consumed to make one drunk—therefore, the wording "not alongside wine." The pastor was not to sit down alongside the very weak wine long enough to consume an amount sufficient to have an effect upon his senses.

10. Read Leviticus 10:8–11. Why did God require that the priests abstain from wine and strong drink?

The application of this requirement to our culture seems obvious. Our wine is so much stronger than wine in Biblical times that even small amounts of it would have much greater effects. The effects upon moral

and spiritual judgment are the most critical and probably the first to occur. Therefore, the pastor of today should not be "alongside wine" at all.

God forbids the pastor to be a "striker," or to hit others physically.
Often such behavior springs from being "soon angry."

11. What Old Testament person had a problem with striking?

Not Loving Silver

The pastor was also not to be "given to filthy lucre" (Titus 1:7). This
requirement parallels 1 Timothy 3:3, which uses a similar word meaning
"not loving silver." The love of money is like a root from which springs
all kinds of evil (1 Timothy 6:9, 10). The pastor who desires money and
schemes to gain it falls into all sorts of trouble.

12. Read Hebrews 13:5. What does God present as the alternative to
covetousness and the reason for contentment?

The Biblical substitute for loving money is dependence upon the
presence of God. God desires pastors who focus on His presence rather
than on profit margins.

Pastors must become lovers of hospitality (v. 8). The word "hospitality" has the idea of loving strangers, but it is also used of loving brothers in Christ. Hospitality includes meeting the spiritual, physical, and
emotional needs of others.

A lover of good men or things is the next qualification (v. 8). A pastor should manifest a tender affection toward people and things that are
of good moral quality.

We limit the word "sober" (v. 8) to nondrunkenness, but it is broader in
meaning, designating one who is sensible and in his right mind. In this context of spiritual qualities, rightmindedness would include thinking as God
thinks or seeing things from God's perspective. The sober pastor looks at
life with a consciousness of distinction between temporal and eternal.

God is the standard for what is right and "just" (v. 8). The pastor must be one with God in what he sees as right, thinking right and making right judgments as he pastors.

Need it be said that devotion to God and everything God calls holy (v. 8) should be a requirement for the pastor? Yes, forgetful humans need reminders.

"Temperance" (v. 8) is self-control. This final aspect of the Spirit's fruit goes against the current of our age (Galatians 5:23). Society reels along, drunken with self-indulgence, while the Spirit-filled pastor walks steadily in the way of self-control.

The pastor is to hold fast the faithful Word (v. 9) as a shipwrecked sailor would to his life preserver. The highest waves of false teaching or opposition cannot sink the pastor who clings to the faithful Word of God. The pastor proclaims truth and opposes falsehood.

13. What practical steps could a church take to determine the degree to which a candidate for leadership has matured in these God-required qualities?

Volumes of Words

Paul's description of the ungodly perfectly fits today's scene (Titus 1:10–16). People abound who do not submit themselves to God's rules, who seek to add meritorious works to God's grace, who speak forth great volumes of words but without real meaning, and who deceive multitudes away from God and into following erroneous humans. They teach what should not be taught, for it is false. Their underlying motivation is money. They must be stopped (vv. 10, 11).

14. What are some examples of leaders like those described in Titus 1:10 and 11?

God's strategy for opposing such people begins with men possessing the spiritual qualities just studied. The word "for" (v. 10) shows that godly leadership is necessary because of the work of ungodly opposition.

15. What often happens when you try to witness to someone who has been turned off to spiritual things by a spiritual leader who fell well short of the Biblical qualifications?

The second part of the Christian response is to have these godly leaders minister the Word of God. They are to rebuke the false teachers sharply (v. 13). The purpose of the rebuke is to make the false leaders become "sound in the faith."

Paul's final description of these ungodly people is chilling. They professed that they knew God when they didn't (v. 16). Such false profession, believed by many, made them more effective in their evil work. However, the many who uncritically accepted their profession of faith should have known better, for their works clearly denied the Lord and thus proved their profession of faith to be false.

Making It Personal

14. Knowing the qualities of godly leaders, what are some things you can do to promote godliness among the leaders of your church?

15. Every adult is a leader in that children look to all adults as examples. Which qualities of godly leadership do you need to work on?

16. What will you do to address that leadership weakness in your life?

17. Memorize Titus 1:5.

Lesson 4

A Godly Lifestyle

*Biblical doctrine leads to a godly
lifestyle in the believer.*

Titus 2:1–10

**"But speak thou the things which become sound
doctrine" (Titus 2:1).**

I magine that you have just purchased the best gift for your
mother—something she has wanted for years. What would
you choose to wrap it in? Yesterday's newspaper? Torn wrapping from a
gift you've received? The best wrapping paper and ribbon you can find?
The store's standard bag for purchases?

Our faith is like a valuable package, and our actions are the wrapping.

Getting Started

1. Why is it important to you that the valuable gift you are giving
looks appealing?

2. What difference would it make to your mother whether the
wrapped gift looks attractive?

Titus 2:1–10 qualifies as one of the most practical sections of God's Word, showing what godly behavior looks like for various groups in the church.

The Relationship of Behavior to Belief

Some things just go together—mashed potatoes and gravy, bacon and eggs, ham and cheese, belief and behavior. The book of Titus shows that wrong beliefs lead to wrong behavior, while good doctrine results in godly behavior.

Titus 1 warned of ungodly people. They professed to know God, although they really did not (v. 16). Discerning believers could have determined the insincerity of these false professors' claims because their behavior denied genuine salvation.

3. Read Acts 26:20. What kind of works should believers do?

4. Read Ephesians 2:10. For what have believers been created in Christ Jesus?

5. Read 1 John 2:4. What does the Bible say about a person who claims to know God but does not obey God's commandments?

When we treat false professors as Christians, we show our lack of urgent concern for their souls. Jesus Christ taught that "by their fruits ye shall know them" (Matthew 7:16, 20).

Chapter 1 of Titus also tells of godly leaders. They held fast to God's faithful Word. And not only were their doctrines good, but their behavior was godly. Sound doctrine led to a godly lifestyle. And this is what Paul instructed Titus to speak about (Titus 2:1).

6. Read 1 John 2:3 and 5. What evidence of knowing God, or assurance of salvation, is mentioned?

A godly lifestyle, or righteous living, is for every Christian. Paul gave Titus examples of the godly lifestyle for five categories of people, beginning with aged Christian men (Titus 2:2).

Aged Men

Sober. Older men are to be fully rational, having conscious control of their total faculties—mind, emotions, and will. The older Christian man is to have a clear perspective about living as God's child in God's creation.

Grave, or dignified. The older Christian man is to be restrained or reverent in his behavior. This dignity of manner comes from a serious attitude toward life. The man can have fun, laugh, and enjoy himself, but at the same time he has an overriding spiritual maturity that knows life is a race, a warfare, a fight.

Temperate. This quality was required of church leaders (Titus 1:8, "sober"). The older man is to have the correct outlook upon God, himself, and all of life.

Sound in the faith. "Faith" in Titus 2:2 may refer to doctrine or to personal trust in God. By virtue of the months and years the older man has daily walked with God, he will have a strong, healthy, robust personal confidence in God and will be well taught in the health-producing truth of the Word.

Sound in love. Love, or "charity," is caring concern. It comes about by an act of the will. It is being interested in another's welfare and disciplining oneself to do what is best for the other. The man who is mature in the faith is not self-centered or self-pitying. He has a genuine concern for others, developed through many years of walking in love as Christ loved us (Ephesians 5:2).

7. Read 1 Corinthians 13:1–3. How important is love for godly Christian living?

Sound in patience. He knows how to persevere and stick to his commitment to Christ, no matter what happens.

8. Read Job 13:15. To what extent was Job determined to persevere in his commitment to God?

Such strong perseverance comes through experience in holding on to Christ through thick and thin. It is easy to lose heart as we get older. We experience increasing physical infirmities and accumulated disappointments. Loneliness grows as friends and family die and we are less able to get around. These things call upon the older Christian to exercise his soundness in patience.

Aged Women

Four characteristics are given to aged Christian women (Titus 2:3).

As becometh holiness. The words "as becometh holiness" mean "as is proper for priests." Older Christian women—indeed all believers today—are priests (1 Peter 2:4, 5). A priest's behavior is primarily that of offering sacrifices.

9. What are the sacrifices of the New Testament priest?

The older Christian woman should be experienced in offering these spiritual sacrifices to God.

Not false accusers. The word translated "accusers" is the Greek word *diabolos.* The same word is translated "devil" and means "a slanderer." A slanderer spreads evil about another for the purpose of hurting that other person.

10. Evaluate this statement: Just one person who spreads evil about others to hurt them could not possibly hurt a church's ministry.

The tongue is very powerful and yet difficult to control, but a mature Christian woman should have learned how to control her tongue by the grace of God.

Not given to much wine. There have been debates over this verse, particularly on the word "much." Why did Paul introduce the concept of much? Because, due to the low alcoholic content of the beverages of that day, it took "much" to dull one's senses, to make one feel different, or to give the relief that addiction craves. Paul emphasized that the women should not be enslaved by wine, and they could not be enslaved by just a little (cf. lesson 3).

Perhaps Paul was not dealing directly with drunkenness here, but with something more subtle. Perhaps he was thinking of that all too prominent practice of older women, and men too, of turning to alcohol for relief from tension, boredom, fear, or loneliness. It's possible for a person to be given to wine and never drink enough at one time to appear drunk. Surely there were those in Paul's day, as today, who drink in the morning to clear their minds, drink at noon to help them face the rest of the day, drink in the evening to relax before dinner, and drink at bedtime for sound sleep. Christian women must not look to a bottle to find strength for living.

Teachers of good things. Paul instructed the older women to tell about good things, explain how the good things fit into everyday life, and encourage others to believe the good things and act upon them. What these good things consist of is revealed in verses 4 and 5 (discussed later). Younger women sat at the feet of the older women to learn those good things. The personal traits required of older women (v. 3) would prepare them to teach others and would make the younger women respect them and be ready to listen to them.

11. Evaluate this statement: Older women and younger women learn best when they are with people their own age.

Young Women

Seven qualities are expected of young Christian women (Titus 2:4, 5). Some apply specifically to married women, while others apply to either single or married women.

To love their husbands. The pressure of today's culture pushes women away from loving their husbands and into loving their own personal fulfillment, which supposedly can be found only away from the husband and the home. The example and encouragement of older Christian women with a track record of tender affection toward their husbands can be a tremendous influence on younger women.

12. How do popular sitcoms often portray a wife's treatment of her husband?

13. What would most sitcom wives think about the Biblical love a wife is supposed to have for her husband?

To love their children. Children can be very lovable in their tender, precious moments. But every mother knows too well those "other" moments. Mothering also involves some tedious chores. If a mother loses sight of her vital role in shaping the character of her children as God's, she can lose her mother's heart of affection.

Be discreet. "Discreet" means to be in one's right mind. The young woman must see life from God's perspective, and not the materialistic or hedonistic perspective of so many of her peers.

Chaste. Purity of life and character bring honor to the Christian woman and to her Lord. Satan attacks the purity of young women today on many fronts, and older women should encourage them in their battle.

14. Read Philippians 4:8. "Pure" here is the same word translated "chaste" in Titus 2:5. How would the instruction in this verse help a person be pure in behavior?

Keepers at home. Literally this expression means "home workers." The idea is first and foremost that the Christian young woman should actively work in the home rather than being lazy or spending time being a busybody. She must not shirk her responsibility to train her children and care for the domestic needs of her family.

Good. Young women, in the prime of health, should be characterized by works that are acceptable to God and beneficial to others.

Obedient to their own husbands. The Greek form probably should be taken in a reflexive sense—she is to submit herself to her husband. God instructs the husband about his duty (love) and the wife about her duty (submit). God does not instruct one mate to force the other to do his or her duty. Each must give an account of himself to God. The wife is responsible to bring herself under the leadership of her own husband.

Young Men

Only one requirement is specified for young Christian men (Titus 2:6). They are to be sober minded. This has already been discussed, as it appeared in 1:8 ("sober), 2:2 ("temperate"), and 2:5 ("discreet").

15. What is the significance of the repetition of this term?

Servants

In Titus 2:9 and 10, the subject changes to the work relationship. The Christian servant-master relationship operated on the basis of principles, many of which apply to employee-employer relationships today.

Obedient. The concept is simple—do what you are told. The difficulty comes when we struggle within for the self-discipline to obey.

Please their masters well. Workers should go beyond mere obedience to orders and think of what would please their masters/employers.

Not answering again (back). Christian workers are not to talk back to or speak against their masters/employers, even behind their backs.

16. Evaluate this statement: Most employees respect their bosses enough to not talk about them behind their backs.

Not purloining. This means they were not to take things that did not belong to them.

17. Have you ever been tempted to take something from work, perhaps just a notepad or package of pens, because you thought your employer owed you? What did you do?

Showing all good fidelity. Christian workers are to show good faith; that is, to be faithful and trustworthy. This includes showing up on time, working instead of surfing the Web, and telling the truth when giving a report to a boss.

Is it really possible for Christian servants/employees to behave this way?

18. Read Colossians 3:22–25. What light do these verses shed on how Christian servants/employees can implement the godly behavior of Titus 2:9 and 10?

Godly Behavior

19. What desecrations (profanities, disrespect, irreverence) are avoided by godly behavior?

The world usually judges Christians by the way they behave, not by what they believe or teach. A godly lifestyle avoids carping criticisms by the world. Note two specific examples. The young women were told that when they behaved as they should, then the Word of God would not be blasphemed (Titus 2:5). And Titus's proper behavior would result in the enemies of the gospel having no evil thing to say of him (v. 8). Both God's Word and God's children are spared bad reviews when His children live lives becoming to sound doctrine.

The word "adorn" (v. 10) in the Greek is *cosmos,* related to our word "cosmetics." It refers to putting things in order so that they look their very best. When we live a godly lifestyle, we adorn the doctrine of God our Savior. Of course, we do not make that doctrine any better than it already is, but we present it in an attractive way. What a privilege to present our Savior's doctrine in the pleasant-looking package of our good conduct. We show the genuineness of the gospel by our good works.

20. In what ways can we live our doctrine before a watching world?

A godly lifestyle facilitates evangelism by removing objections against the Word and against Christians, and by demonstrating that the gospel leads to an attractive way of life.

Making It Personal

Christ's preciousness to believers makes us desire to adorn His doctrine with our godly living (1 Peter 2:7).

21. Review the regulations for your age/gender and praise God for allowing you to honor the Lord by the ones at which you excel.

22. Tell Him of your sincere desire to improve in the ones where you are weaker, and ask Him for special grace to honor Him in those too.

23. Memorize Titus 2:1.

Where Godliness Comes From

*Christ's death makes godly living
possible and desirable.*

Titus 2:11—3:3

"Looking for that blessed hope, and the glorious appearing of the great God and our Saviour Jesus Christ; Who gave himself for us, that he might redeem us from all iniquity, and purify unto himself a peculiar people, zealous of good works" (Titus 2:13, 14).

Suppose you are walking down a sidewalk when you come upon a lady who is frantically searching the grass. You approach her and find out that she is looking for the diamond from her wedding ring. It fell out somewhere within the block. How would you respond?

Now imagine you are walking with your wife or mother when she realizes that the diamond from her wedding ring has just fallen out. How would you respond?

Getting Started

1. Often our motivations rise and fall according to our relationships. How do your relationships normally affect your motivation?

2. Have you ever been suddenly motivated to do something because of a relationship that became part of the picture?

Searching the Scriptures

This lesson stresses the incentive that a relationship with Christ provides to believers to live godly lives.

The Christian is a new creation in Christ (2 Corinthians 5:17). This new creation shows itself in attitudes, values, and actions. Likewise, false professors can be identified by their works that deny God.

The good works required of the Christian are made possible by Jesus Christ and His substitutionary sacrifice on Calvary.

3. What will you succeed in doing if you try to be more spiritual through a self-improvement plan that is based on personal efforts?

Basis for Godliness

Titus 2:11 is one of the most significant Biblical summaries of the gospel of Christ and its effect on one's life. It begins with a reminder that the grace of God has appeared, bringing salvation. God's grace refers to Christ's first coming. He was motivated by the grace of God to come to earth, and He manifested God's grace in an extraordinary way (John 1:14, 17). Therefore, Paul could quite properly refer to the Person of Christ as "the grace of God."

The words "to all men" probably should not be placed with "appeared" but rather with "bringeth salvation." On the one hand, Christ as a man did not appear to all men in His first advent. On the other hand, Paul clearly stated that God is "the Saviour of all men, specially of those that believe" (1 Timothy 4:10).

God is the Savior of all in two senses. First, salvation was provided for all at Calvary. Christ's death was sufficient for all, made provision for all, and is available to all who believe.

Second, Christ's death made possible God's common grace and providential blessing upon all. God does not judge an individual with Hell immediately when he or she sins. Rather, He can be long-suffering, giving the individual time and opportunity to repent (Genesis 15:7, 13–16; Romans 2:4; 2 Peter 3:9). In this limited sense of God's gracious, delayed judgment and many earthly blessings, God is the Savior of all.

4. What do many unbelievers wrongly conclude about God's gracious long-suffering?

The salvation that Christ brought has several facets, in keeping with the many-faceted grace of God. His salvation saves from the penalty of sin so that all condemnation due to sin is removed (Romans 8:1). It also saves from the enslaving power of sin and its various lusts and pleasures (Titus 3:3).

5. Read John 8:34, 36 and Romans 6:12, 14. From what does the Son make one free?

6. Read Romans 6:18 and 22. When God frees a person from serving sin, then to what does that person become a servant?

The salvation of Christ forms the basis for changing one's behavior from sin to godly living. It has made the believer free from the mastery of sin so that he has no obligation or necessity to obey sin, but to be a servant of God. Therefore the Christian should and can reject the solicitations of sin and should have fruit unto holiness. Christ taught that the fruit of godliness could occur only as a person abides in Him, the Vine. Without Him we can do nothing that God considers good or godly (John 15:4, 5).

7. Evaluate this statement: I tried to quit committing a particular sin, but I came to the conclusion that I just can't help it.

More Godly Behaviors

The Christian who studies the book of Titus can never say he was ignorant of how God wanted him to behave. God made His expectations crystal clear.

The grace of God, in the Person of Christ, teaches believers (Titus 2:12). You might say that Christians are enrolled in the school of God's grace. Jesus Christ teaches two principles that are basic to Christian living: deny (don't do) and live (do).

Ungodliness and worldly lusts must be denied. The believer who meditates continuously in God's Word experiences a growing respect and appreciation for God. As a result, he will deny ungodliness when it seeks a place in his attitudes.

8. What happens in your life as you decrease your daily intake of God's Word?

Unsaved people willingly and unwittingly do the desires of the devil, all the while thinking themselves free (John 8:32–34). Their desires are so typical of this world that "worldly desires" is a fitting title. These desires seldom go beyond temporal circumstances and material possessions. The believer must deny such limited and misdirected desires from lodging in his or her thoughts.

9. What might you say to someone who doesn't want to become a Christian because he doesn't want someone to tell him what to do?

Our denial of ungodliness and worldly lusts creates the atmosphere in which living a Christlike life is possible.

10. What three words would you use to describe the life God wants us to live?

11. Read Titus 2:12. What three words did Paul use to describe the proper way to live?

"Soberly" has to do with proper thoughts and having the eternal perspective (1:8; 2:2, "temperate;" 2:5, "discreet"). "Righteously" has to do with behavior that is right in God's eyes because it conforms to His righteous standards. "Godly" describes an attitude that holds God in high esteem. These three terms describe godliness in a general sense.

Believers are to separate themselves from the sinful practices, attitudes, and values of the world; but at the same time, they are to be very much involved with the lost people of the world for the purpose of outreach (John 17:11, 14). At the beginning of Titus 3, Paul wrote directions for the Christian in relationship to the government and society at large.

Government

The Christian should "be subject to" the government (Titus 3:1), which indicates a voluntary submitting in general. But specifically, those in authority are to be obeyed (cf. Romans 13:1–7; 1 Timothy 2:2; 1 Peter 2:13–17). However, obedience to human rulers is not absolute, for they sometimes require things that God specifically forbids, or they forbid things that God specifically requires (cf. Acts 1:8; 5:28, 29).

12. What are some laws that could pass in the near future that would be contrary to what God requires of us as believers?

Society

The Christian's responsibilities to society include three items named in Titus 3:1b and 2. First, be ready to do every good work. God created us in Christ for good works (Ephesians 2:10).

13. Read Galatians 6:10. What should you do if you have an opportunity to do good to a person, but you just don't like the person?

Second, the Christian is not to speak evil of any man (Titus 3:2).
The two words "speak evil" could be translated "blaspheme." All people
have been made in the image of God; and even though that image has
been badly marred by sin, every human being still bears it. Therefore,
to blaspheme another human being is to attack the image of God in
him. This must not be done (James 3:9–11).

Third, we are not to be brawlers, but peaceable (Titus 3:2). The depraved
mind frequently looks to physical force or violence as a solution to problems.
Both the good guys and the bad guys seem to take care of difficulties with
their fists or their guns. But the Christian is not to be a fighter ("brawler").

The final word contains an alternative to brawling. The believer
should display gentleness (v. 2). Gentle actions arise from a meek spirit.
Jesus Christ displayed meekness by His gentleness (2 Corinthians 10:1).

14. Read Galatians 5:22 and 23. What would you say to someone
who says his personality is such that he cannot be gentle?

Treating offensive people with gentleness tries one's soul. But Christians have good reason to be gentle. We should remember that we for-
merly behaved offensively, especially toward God (Titus 3:3). And how
did God treat us, offenders who are now saved? With kindness and love
(v. 4ff.). Therefore, as God's representatives, we Christians should treat
unsaved people as God treated us when we were unsaved.

Christ's Death

Jesus Christ came once to seek and to save the lost. For what purposes
was His death intended? Titus 2:13–15 mentions two of God's purposes.

First, Christ died to redeem us from all iniquity (v. 14). The word "iniquity" here means "lawlessness," or "violations of God's laws." Sin is the
transgression of the law. Christ died to pay the penalty of sin and thereby
purchase us for Himself. After He has bought us, He has plans for us, and
those plans are found in the second purpose mentioned in the text.

The second purpose of Christ's death was to purify unto Himself a people obviously His and zealous of good works (v. 14). It was intended to revolutionize our manner of life on earth. The believer demonstrates God's ownership by being zealous to do what is good in God's sight.

15. What are some evidences of being zealous for good works?

Christ's Coming

Jesus Christ will appear in the future (Titus 2:13). Certain descriptions of Him emphasize His character as it will be shown in the blessed-hope appearing.

First, He will appear as God. He truly is both God and man; but during His first appearing, His deity seldom shown through the veil of His humanity. Christ's deity clearly radiated forth at the Transfiguration, but that was not typical of His earthly form.

Second, He will appear as our Savior, which calls to mind His suffering to the point of death at Calvary ("gave Himself," v. 14). The Savior Who will appear is the Savior Who saved us from all iniquity and unto Himself that we should be uniquely His possession ("a peculiar people") and should manifest His character in our lives ("zealous of good works"). So, one of God's purposes at Calvary was to save people who would be pure, obviously God's possession, and doing good works with great zeal when Christ returns.

16. How can we increase our awareness of the coming of Christ so that it provides us with a greater incentive for godly living?

Expecting Jesus—Who expects sanctified living and Who suffered crucifixion to enable it—naturally motivates a Christian to such living.

Strong Teaching

Titus was to be continually speaking this message of godliness, its basis, its description, and its incentive (Titus 2:15). However, merely teaching these things would not be enough. Titus was to urge the Cretans strongly, perhaps in messages and also in personal encounters. He would work with people to help the weak implement godly living.

Some people would need even more than urging. After much exhortation, they would still stray from godly living. Such people Titus was to rebuke, pointing out the error of their ways.

Sad to say, constant teaching, exhortation, and even rebuke would fail to impress some, because they would view Titus's message as merely his own opinions. Therefore, he was to teach, exhort, and rebuke with authority. All the authority of the apostle Paul stood behind the message of Titus, and all the authority of Jesus Christ stood behind Paul's message. Therefore, the churches were to take Titus quite seriously. He was not to allow them to disregard his words. These messages of godliness are urgent messages. The Christians of Crete needed to be impressed with them, and so do we.

Making It Personal

17. What are you genuinely excited about: your favorite sports team, seeing your children do well, a vacation to your favorite hideaway? How does your zeal for good works compare with the other things you just considered?

18. Spend time each day thinking about a good thing or two God wants you to do, and then save a place on your calendar to get it done in appreciation for the day Christ died for you.

19. What if Christ returned today? What would you want to do to get ready?

20. Do that now, for He may indeed return today. Live every day as if Christ was on His way—for He is!

21. Memorize Titus 2:13 and 14.

Lesson 6

Godliness in Action

*Believers benefit from being careful
to maintain good works.*

Titus 3:4–15

**"This is a faithful saying, and these things I will
that thou affirm constantly, that they which
have believed in God might be careful to maintain good works. These things are good and
profitable unto men" (Titus 3:8).**

Henry Ward Beecher said, "As flowers always wear their own colors and give forth their own fragrance every day alike, so should Christians maintain their character at all times and under all circumstances." Or at least we are supposed to. Maintaining behaviors to which we have committed ourselves is not always easy.

Getting Started

1. What factors make it difficult to maintain behaviors to which we have committed ourselves?

2. What would you say is the most challenging factor?

51

Believers are to be godly because God is godly (1 Peter 1:15, 16).

God's Actions

God's actions are godly simply because He does them. God is the standard by which every being and activity must be judged. One way in which fallen man seeks to be God is by making himself the standard for his own behavior and claiming to be unaccountable to anyone outside of himself.

God's moral perfections make Him a perfect moral standard. God does not capriciously decide what is right and wrong. His independence from outside authority does not result in a tyranny, for He operates in perfect harmony with His own internal standards. God's attributes are infinitely perfect, and all that He does harmonizes with the totality of His attributes. For example, the seeming opposites of justice and mercy both play their proper roles in any decision God makes regarding a disobedient creature. Our God is a great God!

3. Read Hosea 14:9. What word describes the Lord's ways?

4. What attitude toward God's ways does it take to simply "walk in them"?

Their root

God's actions in providing salvation for us spring from His attributes of kindness, love, and mercy (Titus 3:4, 5a). The New Testament stresses that Jesus Christ epitomizes God's kindness (Ephesians 2:7). Through Jesus Christ, God's kindness has come to us. Christ's appearance on earth may be called the appearance of the kindness of our Savior (Titus 3:4).

5. What are some examples of Jesus' good works of kindness that He performed while on earth?

Next Paul cited God's love. Two primary Greek words for love, agape and phileo, appear many times in the New Testament. Agape love is more objective love; it is more related to the will. We may call it caring concern. Agape love looks at the object loved, and out of concern for the object's well-being, it decides to do what it can for the loved one. The focus is on the one loved.

Phileo love is more subjective love. It is more related to the emotions. We could call it tender affection. Phileo love looks at the object loved, and out of warm feelings for the object, it moves into action. The focus is on both the one loving and the one loved.

The love of God that appeared in the Person of Christ was agape, according to John 3:16, but also phileo love, according to Titus 3:4. God has been both concerned about us and affectionate toward us. What encouraging thoughts!

6. How do you feel when someone says that he loves you but his actions toward you scream that he doesn't?

God says that He loves us and that all of His actions, whether we understand them or not, are done in love toward us.

7. Why is it wrong to determine whether or not God loves you based on whether or not He brings about beneficial circumstances on your behalf?

Finally, Paul referred to God's attribute of mercy, or His compassion for those who are suffering. Believers can trust in the mercy of God forever and ever (Psalm 52:8). God saved us according to His mercy (Titus 3:5). His actions in Titus 3:4–15 arise from His kindness, love, and mercy.

Their Reality

God has acted in saving us. In Titus 3:5 Paul described salvation in terms of the washing of regeneration and renewing of the Holy Spirit.

Sin defiles like an irremovable stain. Only God can provide a cleansing agent powerful enough to remove the defilements of sin. The blood of Christ is His effective sin-stain remover. Regeneration brings a washing from sin's defilement that leaves the born-again babe in Christ spotless. Such flawless perfection goes beyond mere repair.

8. Would you eat directly off the bathroom floor in your house even if you cleaned it first? Why or why not?

Nothing we clean on earth is ever completely clean like the regenerated heart of a believer.

The word "regeneration" literally means "born again." The noun is used of individual salvation only here in the New Testament. Jesus and Nicodemus engaged in a detailed discussion of this concept (John 3). Jesus' words there reveal the Holy Spirit's active role in making a person to be born again. Regeneration is rightly called a renewing by the Holy Spirit.

Since God alone can produce the new birth in an individual, being born again may be described as being born of God (1 John 3:9; 4:7). God begets us with the word of truth (James 1:18). The Word of God produces faith like a seed produces a plant (Romans 10:17; 1 Peter 1:23), and faith is the channel by which one receives the new birth. The Holy Spirit of God accomplishes regeneration using the Word of God.

9. Read Titus 3:5. When have you sensed the power of the Holy Spirit in an obvious way in your life?

Holy Spirit's Enabling

God has also acted in giving believers the Holy Spirit Himself (Titus 3:6). During Jesus' earthly ministry, the Holy Spirit dwelt with the disciples, but He was not dwelling in them (John 14:17). The Holy Spirit came on the Day of Pentecost (Acts 2). At that time the He also took up permanent residence in every believer, as Christ had said He would.

Now every believer is a temple of the Holy Spirit (1 Corinthians 6:19).

10. Read Titus 3:6. What would you say to the person who complains that he or she can't do anything for the Lord?

Paul also mentioned that God's salvation includes being justified (Titus 3:7). This word may sound complicated at first, but it simply means "to declare one righteous." When the publicans justified God (Luke 7:29), they declared that God was righteous. When God justifies a sinner, He declares that sinner righteous by virtue of Christ's righteousness being imputed to him (2 Corinthians 5:21).

Finally, God has acted in making us heirs (Titus 3:7). His long-range purpose in saving us included a grand inheritance. Many of salvation's blessings fall into our hands while we still inhabit the earth, but others will not be seen until we arrive at home in Heaven (1 Peter 1:4).

11. Read Titus 3:7. What would you say to the believer who says he is a nobody and has no future?

Christians rejoice over God's actions of saving, giving the Holy Spirit, and providing an inheritance. Such actions conform to His character and lie exclusively within His ability. Such actions by God are truly good works.

Maintain

The exhortation to good works appears twice in the final verses of Titus (Titus 3:8–11). Those who have believed in God must maintain good works. To do so, an individual must rule over self to see that good works constantly get accomplished. The flesh tends away from good works, but God's will is for all who have believed to maintain good works throughout their lives.

12. What are some examples of good works that are readily available for most believers to do?

13. Evaluate this statement: I would have gotten involved in good works if someone had asked me to get involved.

14. Read Titus 3:14. Maintaining good works prevents what condition?

Verse 8 implies that maintaining good works can slip from our conscious thoughts unless we are "careful," that is, take definite steps to think about doing them. Verse 14 informs us that we must learn to maintain good works. Ruling over ourselves to constantly maintain good works doesn't just happen automatically. The maintenance of good works results from careful thought and personal education.

15. Read Titus 3:8. What could you do practically to make sure you maintain good works?

16. In addition to pleasing God, how are good works good and profitable to the doer and his peers?

We must discern a most important sequence in the text. First, one must be saved by faith, "not by works of righteousness which we have done" (v. 5). Following salvation, "they which have believed in God" must be careful to lead lives full of good works (v. 8). Salvation is first, then good works; not the reverse.

Avoid

Separation means keeping close to the holy God as well as keeping apart from all that is evil. Christians walking the path of godliness find the highway has warning signs against certain exits or side roads. The pilgrim must avoid foolish questions, genealogies, and contentions and strivings about the law.

These types of questions are pointless and often deal with the hypothetical. Those who ask such questions are often attempting to undermine the Bible so they can ease their consciences that are pricking them to submit to the truth of the Word.

17. Read Titus 3:9. How do these questions contrast sharply with good works?

18. What would happen to a pastor's ministry if he spent a lot of time trying to answer foolish questions?

Works-righteousness appeals to the flesh. The Jews of the Old Testament times fell into the snare of thinking God would be pleased by their external conformity to the rituals of the law. Although salvation has always been and will always be received on the basis of faith, the Jews turned the sacrifices and other required behaviors into a works-righteousness system whereby one supposedly received salvation by doing.

Judaism in New Testament times had become a perversion of God's revealed system. And Jewish teachers crept into the churches, claiming to believe in Christ but still insisting on the necessity of works to obtain or to maintain one's salvation. They were known as Judaizers. Titus and his learners were to avoid, shun, or stay away from the Judaizers' foolish questions, genealogies, and contentions and strivings about the law

Reject

Heretics are those who have chosen doctrine contrary to sound doctrine, and who, therefore, cause divisions over doctrine because their followers disagree with those who hold the truth. (See 1 Corinthians 11:18 and 19 and 2 Peter 2:1 for the subject of heresy.)

The Christian must reject heretics, for they have turned aside from God (are subverted); they are sinning (missing the mark of God's truth); and their teaching shows them to be under condemnation by God (Titus 3:11). However, the Christian is to warn the heretic of his dangerous position, hoping that he will repent (2 Timothy 2:24–26). In fact, two warnings must precede the rejection of the person of the heretic (Titus 3:10).

19. What is the danger in ignoring a heretic in your church?

Titus's Actions

Paul closed his letter to Titus with personal instructions to his representative. Three godly behaviors awaited Titus's doing. First he was to visit Paul. Paul had assigned Titus to Crete and the establishment of the Cretan churches (Titus 1:5). Paul decided to spend the winter (a difficult time for travel) at Nicopolis, and he desired Titus's presence (Titus 3:12). Either Artemas or Tychicus would take Titus's place in Crete.

Second, Titus was to give missionary support to the team of Zenas and Apollos (v. 13). Perhaps these two missionaries were Paul's couriers to take his letter to Titus.

Finally, Titus was to give Paul's greetings to all those who loved him in the faith (v. 15).

We have seen that godly living comes from the enabling of God, not merely by self-determination. However, there must be that personal decision to follow after godliness and to call upon the resources provided by the Lord if a believer is to make progress or growth in holy living.

Making It Personal

20. List five benefits from doing good works, benefits you have already experienced or aspire to experience.

21. Resolve with God that you will be thoughtful to maintain good works.

22. Memorize Titus 3:8.

Lesson 7

Faithful Servants

Faithful servants of God must be servants of faith.

2 Timothy 1:1–8

"Be not thou therefore ashamed of the testimony of our Lord, nor of me his prisoner; but be thou partaker of the afflictions of the gospel according to the power of God" (2 Timothy 1:8).

For years college students have lacked adequate sleep, living like zombies or perked up with caffeine. Students have even bragged about their few hours of rest. But recent studies have shown that sleep deprivation is related to poor academic performance. So universities are trying to promote better sleep habits, some using slogans like, "Want A's? Get Z's." Adequate sleep is a prerequisite for academic success.

Getting Started

1. What are some prerequisites for being a faithful servant of God?

2. What would be a catchy slogan to promote faithful service to God?

61

Searching the Scriptures

Paul, the Writer

Years before Paul wrote 2 Timothy, God had laid hold of Saul of Tarsus on the Damascus Road. And through the messenger Ananias in Damascus, He told Saul that he was to be an apostle to the Greeks and to kings, as well as to the Children of Israel (Acts 9:15). Saul, who is also called Paul, was an apostle of Christ by the will of God (2 Timothy 1:1; Galatians 2:8). He did not appoint himself to that role, nor did any human authority appoint him.

3. Read 2 Timothy 1:8. What did Paul mean by calling himself the Lord's prisoner?

Paul reminisced as he sat chained in prison. Note how many times memory is mentioned. Paul had memories of Timothy (2 Timothy 1:3), of Timothy's tears (v. 4), and of the faith that Timothy and his forebears possessed (v. 5). Paul even wanted to stir up some memories in Timothy's mind (v. 6).

4. What faithful servants of God do you reminisce about every so often?

Timothy, the Reader

Timothy, whose name means "honoring God" or "honored by God," accompanied Paul during periods of his missionary journeys. Paul apparently led Timothy to Christ (1 Timothy 1:2). Timothy had such a good reputation in Lystra that Paul recruited him to join the team (Acts 16:3).

Sometimes Timothy traveled with Paul, while at other times Paul moved on from a city, leaving Timothy behind to build up the believers (1 Timothy 1:3). Paul also would send Timothy to a church as his personal messenger (1 Corinthians 4:17; 1 Thessalonians 3:1, 2) or summon Timothy to join him (2 Timothy 4:21). Timothy, with others, accompanied Paul on his way to Jerusalem after the third missionary journey (Acts 20:4, 5).

Timothy was with Paul in Rome during his house arrest, when Paul wrote Philemon (Philemon 1). In fact, the two ministered together so often that Paul mentioned Timothy as the joint sender in six of his epistles. Timothy and Paul were also uniquely like-minded regarding their concern for ministry and for churches (Philippians 2:19–23). They formed an effective and faithful ministry team.

5. What are some other ministry teams, perhaps a husband and wife, who have worked well together for years through good times and bad?

Servants of Faith

6. Read 2 Timothy 1:5. What was in Timothy, Eunice, and Lois?

The faith of Timothy; his mother, Eunice; and his grandmother, Lois came to Paul's mind. Paul described their faith as an "unfeigned" faith. Paul's word "unfeigned" could be translated "unhypocritical."

7. What are some evidences that a person has a genuine faith?

Timothy's faith was from the heart. It was sincere and genuine. He was not playing a role when he claimed to believe in Jesus Christ. Likewise, his mother and her mother before her believed in God sincerely.

8. Read 1 Corinthians 4:17. How did Paul describe Timothy, his beloved son?

9. What description, if any, could be more complimentary for Timothy?

Second Timothy focuses upon the subject of faithfulness to God. We must understand clearly that faith in God has to precede faithfulness to God. One must exercise saving faith before he can faithfully walk with God. Timothy had faith and was faithful.

Servants of Faithfulness

Paul lived a faithful, though difficult, life for Christ. He suffered much persecution. But certainly when he died, the Savior greeted him with the coveted "Well done, thou good and faithful servant," for he was faithful to the end. Paul's faithfulness in serving and in praying are seen in this section of Scripture.

Paul had a heritage for which to be thankful (2 Timothy 1:3). He learned about God from his ancestors, and he served God as a believer with a personal relationship with Christ. It was a blessing for Paul to have grown up as a Jew with knowledge of Jehovah rather than as a pagan who served false gods. After Paul became a Christian, he continued to serve God with the kind of wholehearted dedication that enabled him to say that he served God with a pure conscience (v. 3).

10. Read 2 Timothy 4:7. What value, if any, could you assign to Paul's finishing his course and keeping the faith?

Paul left us a commendable example of serving God faithfully. He also left one of praying. Paul prayed for Timothy without ceasing. Certainly that brought a response from God on Timothy's behalf, and the knowledge of Paul's prayers would have comforted the young man.

11. Read 1 Thessalonians 5:17. What connection do you see between 1 Thessalonians 5:17 and 2 Timothy 1:3?

12. How might knowing that you have a faithful believer praying for you affect you?

Paul had a great desire to be reunited with Timothy. Whenever he thought of being with Timothy, he remembered Timothy's tears, probably the tears Timothy had shed when he and Paul parted company (2 Timothy 1:4). Many in our culture think it is not manly to cry and that men should not show emotions. Here a real man of God cried. Christian men need to be strong in their stand for what is right and brave in warfare for Christ, but at the same time compassionate, tender, and gentle. Jesus Himself was known for His meekness and gentleness. In 1 Timothy 3:3 Paul instructed that the leaders of the church must be gentle ("patient"). Undoubtedly, the emotional ties between Paul and Timothy enhanced their mutual prayers for each other.

Stir up the Gift

Paul, the elder warrior, knew the suffering and secret of faithfulness. The younger Timothy needed encouragement in this precious character quality. So Paul put Timothy in remembrance to stir up the gift of God that was in him by the putting on of his hands (2 Timothy 1:6). The gift that Timothy possessed is not identified in Scripture, so we cannot be sure what it was. It may refer to the office that he had been given, the ministry of service among the churches as in Ephesians 4:11, or it may have reference to the enabling that God had given him to carry out his ministry; that is, a spiritual gift, as found in Romans 12:6–8 and 1 Corinthians 12—14.

13. Read 1 Peter 4:10 and 11. What do these verses teach about faithfully ministering the gift God has given us?

Paul exhorted Timothy to stir up his gift as one would make a fire burn brightly by stirring it. Paul was not implying that Timothy had neglected the gift or let it die down. The present tense, "be stirring," meant that he should continually be stirring up the gift and faithfully exercising it for the glory of Christ.

Timothy had this gift by the putting on of Paul's hands. Paul had told Timothy in an earlier letter not to neglect the gift that was given to him by prophecy (1 Timothy 4:14). Some who had the gift of prophecy announced that Timothy had been appointed by God to a certain ministry or to have certain gifts for ministry. The group realized that God had ordained Timothy to serve Him. They accepted those prophetic words and identified with Timothy by laying hands on him (2 Timothy 1:6). The word "presbytery" is a Greek word meaning "elders." Probably the elders of the church at Ephesus gathered around Timothy and put their hands on him, recognizing God's call and identifying with him in the work of the Lord. Timothy, remembering his gift and his ordination, was to serve Christ faithfully day after day.

Paul also knew Timothy's personality and tendencies. His inner spirit needed encouragement, and Paul encouraged him not to be afraid. Fear should not keep us from exercising our abilities and fulfilling our ministry for Christ. In contrast to a spirit of fear, the Christian has been provided power, love, and a sound mind (2 Timothy 1:7).

14. Read Ephesians 1:18–20. What two historical displays of God's power illustrate His power toward believers, the power that works in us?

15. What can't take the place of God's power when it comes to serving Him faithfully?

Timothy need not fear with such power on his side, and neither do we today need to fear.

The power did not stand alone. God accompanied it with love (v. 7). Love for God and the lost doesn't come naturally. That kind of love flows from God through us. If we love ourselves, then we will stop serving God the moment any discomfort arises.

16. What is God's servant able to do because he or she has God's love?

Timothy had the love of God in him that would motivate him to love the lost even though it would cause him suffering.

God also gave a spirit of a sound mind, or self-control, self-discipline, or good judgment. Rather than being fearful in the Lord's service, Timothy was to remember that God is in control. Rather than allowing fear to carry him away into timid withdrawal, he should exercise self-discipline and faithfully serve God.

17. Why is a "sound mind," or a spirit of self-control and calm, needed in serving the Lord?

What was it that made Timothy fearful in his service? It was an underlying sense of shame. Jesus Christ said that it was possible to be ashamed of Him (Mark 8:38). Paul testified that he was not ashamed of the gospel of Christ (Romans 1:16), and he urged Timothy not to be ashamed of the testimony of the Lord. Nor should Timothy be ashamed of Paul, the Lord's prisoner. It would have been easy for Timothy to be ashamed of a man who was in jail and about to be executed. If Timothy were ashamed and fearful, then he would recoil from faithful service to Christ. If he were not ashamed or fearful, then he would boldly go forth in his ministry for Christ.

Should Timothy boldly live for, serve, and proclaim Christ, persecution would come his way. Notice the strong contrast found in 2 Timothy 1:8. Be not ashamed, but (strong word) be a partaker of the afflictions of the gospel according to the power of God. A hostile world brings affliction upon those who tell it the good news of Christ.

Paul did not hide those afflictions. He did not dupe Timothy into thinking all would be smooth when he served the Lord. He said to serve the Lord and partake of the afflictions that go with the gospel in the power of God. The gospel itself is the power of God (Romans 1:16). As Timothy realized that the gospel was the power of God and as he proclaimed it, he would suffer in accordance with the powerful gospel that he proclaimed. Also, as he proclaimed it, God would use it to bring others to eternal life, and perhaps He would even use the suffering accompanying its proclamation to influence others for Christ. Finally, God might even miraculously deliver Timothy from certain sufferings, as He did with Peter and others, and in that way manifest His power.

Timothy was to take part in the afflictions of the gospel in accordance with the power of God—His power innate in the gospel, His power to save others even through the testimony of suffering saints, and His power to deliver suffering saints as He so chooses.

Making It Personal

18. If the apostle Paul were to write a statement describing your faithfulness, what would it be?

19. What can you do to become more faithful in your service for the Lord?

20. Memorize 2 Timothy 1:8.

Faithfulness in History

*Examples both of faithfulness and failure
motivate us to be faithful.*

2 Timothy 1:9—2:2

"For the which cause I also suffer these things: nevertheless I am not ashamed: for I know whom I have believed, and am persuaded that he is able to keep that which I have committed unto him against that day" (2 Timothy 1:12).

Betsy Chalmers of Richmond, Virginia, believes in faithfulness. She says, "I met him when I was 19, married him at 20 and we were separated when I turned 22 because he was arrested for and then convicted of a violent crime. . . . I stayed through weeks of trials, years in jail and decades in prison. . . . I am now 50. He is 55. He is still my husband and my best friend. I see him four hours every weekend and I talk to him on the phone twice a week for 20 minutes. I am not deceived or a martyr. I am not stupid, uneducated or desperate. I am a wife" (www.npr.org/templates/story/story.php?storyId=5619291).

Getting Started

1. Give an example of faithfulness in your own life.

2. What motivated you to remain faithful?

3. What challenges did you face in remaining faithful?

Searching the Scriptures

Our previous lesson looked at two faithful servants of God, Paul and Timothy. These same two men dominate this lesson, which demonstrates faithfulness through several examples and then encourages faithfulness in Timothy, and in believers today.

Faithfulness par excellence resides in God Himself, and so Paul began with a mention of God's faithfulness in salvation. Verses 9 and 10 of 2 Timothy 1 also form a transition from the reference to the gospel (v. 8) to the present section.

Planning Salvation

God saves people, and in saving them, He calls them to holy living (2 Timothy 2:9).

4. Read 2 Timothy 1:9. How does being called to holiness relate to faithfulness?

God's salvation is not according to human works but according to His own purpose and grace (v. 9). The Bible is clear that no one is ever saved on the basis of works, either carried out or foreseen (Ephesians 2:8, 9).

The basis of God's saving and calling was His own purpose and grace (2 Timothy 2:9). God's purpose to save was given to the ones chosen in Christ "before the world began," which literally means "before times of ages," or "before eternal times." Before there were any eras or successive ages of time, God in His grace decided to save lost people.

5. How does God's choosing you for salvation before time even began help you see your need to be faithful?

Providing Salvation

The purpose and grace of God, established before the world began, had been somewhat hidden down through the ages. That is not to say that they were absolutely hidden, for the Old Testament revealed many of God's purposes and much of God's grace.

Yet it was only in Christ's actual arrival and His death on the cross that the saving purposes of God and His grace were so fully made known, or manifest (2 Timothy 1:10). Paul spoke about the mystery that had been hidden from ages and from generations but in his day was made manifest to God's saints (Colossians 1:26). And John informed the first-century Christians that the law was given by Moses, but grace and truth came by Jesus Christ (John 1:17). The appearing of the Savior in His first advent made the purposes and grace of God more fully manifest.

When Christ came, He abolished death (2 Timothy 1:10). Obviously He did not cause death to become extinct, nor did He annihilate it, for it still painfully exists. The idea of the word "abolished" is that He rendered it powerless, broke its control or loosened the hold that it had. Death has been reduced to the place where Christians who are dead can be referred to as merely sleeping (1 Thessalonians 4:13ff.). It has been so changed that it can be referred to as gain, for to die is to depart and be with Christ (Philippians 1:21, 23). It is significant that these bold words about Christ's having abolished death were written by Paul while he faced imminent death!

6. Read Matthew 5:18. How does this verse relate to the faithfulness of God and His Word?

7. Read Malachi 3:6. How does this truth about God relate to His faithfulness?

8. Which of God's promises about the future as revealed in His Word are you looking forward to seeing fulfilled the most?

Paul's Faithfulness

Paul had been appointed a preacher and an apostle and a teacher of the gospel (2 Timothy 1:11).

9. Read 2 Timothy 1:11. Who ultimately appointed Paul to the ministries listed in this verse?

10. What are possible dangers in serving as if a person or group of people ultimately appointed you to ministry?

The honored position of preacher, apostle, and teacher of the gospel earned Paul opposition. He said that because he faithfully proclaimed the gospel as God's preacher, apostle, and teacher, he also suffered "these things," meaning imprisonment and impending death.

In spite of the suffering, Paul gave Timothy a word of encouragement. Paul revealed the source of the boldness that kept him going on for God. He knew Whom he had believed (2 Timothy 1:12). Paul knew his Savior, his Lord, his God.

11. Read Philippians 3:10. What had been Paul's great desire?

12. Evaluate this statement: A person can be saved for forty years and still not know God very well.

Paul's experiential knowledge of God gained by a daily walk with Christ created firm convictions. Those convictions were that He is really God, that the gospel is really true, and that it is worth continuing on God's side even though the heat gets intense. Paul knew Whom he had believed (2 Timothy 1:12).

Since Paul knew God experientially, he was persuaded that God could guard, keep, preserve, or protect that which he had committed to Him. The phrase "that which I have committed unto him" literally says "the deposit of me."

Most likely, the deposit that Paul was talking about was himself; that is, he had deposited himself or committed himself to God. This is in harmony with the idea of 1 Peter 4:19 that those who suffer should commit the keeping of their souls to God as unto a faithful Creator.

13. How should knowing that we are deposited with God and cannot be "withdrawn" for any reason affect our lives?

14. How should it not affect our lives?

Paul deposited himself in the bank of Heaven. God, the Banker and Guard, would keep the deposit safe and sound until that Day of Judgment. Then the deposit, Paul himself, would be called for, and God would produce it and give it to Jesus Christ, the Judge. If Paul were to be protected from fatal tampering by Satan, if he were to be held safe in the Father's hands until the Judgment Seat of Christ, then he had nothing to fear from persecution. Even though the enemies of the gospel might take his life, his soul would remain unscathed. This assurance from God prevented Paul from being ashamed of his commission or his situation.

Unfaithful Ones

Not everyone is faithful. God is faithful in the absolute sense. Paul had been faithful, but others had not. Timothy knew by personal experience that all they "who are in Asia" had turned away from Paul (2 Timothy 1:15). How are Paul's words here to be understood? Obviously there were, at the very time Paul wrote, believers in Asia who had not turned away from him. Specifically, there were believers in Ephesus who had not turned away from Paul, and Timothy himself was one of them.

Second Timothy 4:16 gives some insight into what Paul meant. There he said that at his first hearing or trial before Caesar, no one stood with him but all forsook him. So in chapter 1, Paul may have been referring to people from Asia who had been with him in Rome at the time of his first trial. These people apparently were ashamed of Paul, Christ's prisoner. They forsook him. Since the time of his trial, they had returned to Asia; as Paul wrote to Timothy, they were back in Asia, and Paul could say that all who were in Asia turned against him.

Unfaithfulness is a very real and present danger. We dare not relax in this area of Christian relationships or be critical of others while we make excuses for ourselves.

15. Read Hebrews 11:32–39. Both the first group, whom God delivered out of their difficulties, and the second group, whom He allowed to suffer, remained faithful and so "obtained a good report" from God. How did they do it?

Onesiphorus' Faithfulness

Paul proceeded to give an example of another faithful person, Onesiphorus (2 Timothy 1:16–18). Onesiphorus had been faithful to Paul, the Lord's servant, both at Ephesus and at Rome.

Onesiphorus often "refreshed" Paul; that is, he cooled him or soothed him (v. 16). We can only speculate as to whether this was physical, emotional, spiritual, or all three. Furthermore, he was not ashamed of Paul's chains.

Onesiphorus had ministered to Paul in some unspecified way when

Paul was at Ephesus. Timothy knew what forms that ministry took, for he had been present in Ephesus when Onesiphorus performed it. So the reference to unspecified ministries by Onesiphorus would have had special significance to Timothy.

Onesiphorus' ministry to Paul at Rome was really an extension of his ministry earlier at Ephesus. When Onesiphorus came to Rome, he sought Paul diligently (v. 17). Paul was locked away in a damp dungeon, and it was difficult for anyone to locate him. Onesiphorus had to cut through government red tape to learn where Paul was sequestered. But he sought Paul with such great diligence that he found him. Certainly Paul was refreshed when this man arrived.

16. Read 2 Timothy 1:17. What are two words that we might use to describe Onesiphorus?

Paul desired that the Lord would give mercy to Onesiphorus' household and to Onesiphorus himself because of his faithful service (2 Timothy 18). Just as Paul had committed himself to the safekeeping of God until the Day of Judgment, so he committed Onesiphorus to the mercy of God until that same climactic event.

17. Read 1 Peter 1:7. How does Christ's future appearing help us be faithful now?

Timothy Charged

The examples of both faithfulness and unfaithfulness form the setting in which Paul charged Timothy to be faithful.

First, Timothy was to be faithful to and to hold fast "the form of sound words" (2 Timothy 1:13). "Form" means a model, standard, or pattern. "Sound words" refers to sound teaching or doctrine. Such teaching is healthful, for that is what the word "sound" means. Timothy received sound words from the apostle Paul. Those words were healthful themselves and produced health in those who received them.

Spiritual health depends on healthy doctrine. Paul had given Timothy the Word of God, and he urged Timothy to hold fast, or cling to, or faithfully stick with orthodoxy (v. 14). How important sound doctrine is in God's sight!

18. Evaluate: Our church doesn't emphasize doctrine because it ends up dividing us and hurting our overall ministry.

19. What are some practical ways a church can guard its doctrine?

While holding fast to sound doctrine is vitally important, Paul went on to say that the manner in which one holds faithfully to sound doctrine is also important. The correct manner for holding fast sound words is "in faith and love" (v. 13). Cold, dead orthodoxy falls short of God's desire. Our orthodoxy must be alive with a living faith and a heartwarming love.

Verse 13 speaks of the manner of maintaining orthodoxy, and verse 14 speaks of the method. Timothy was to be faithful in doctrine. The Holy Spirit teaches what sound doctrine is, and He enables a believer to guard and keep it.

Second, Timothy was also to be strong in grace (2 Timothy 2:1). "Be strong" is a present tense command, meaning to do a deed immediately and continually. "Grace" in Scripture often speaks of the attribute of God that provides undeserved blessings. It is also used to speak of the blessings of God that His attribute supplies. His gifts of grace are sometimes simply called His grace. Paul instructed Timothy to remain faithful by being strong in the blessings of God's grace—the power, the love, the sound mind (v. 7).

Third, Timothy was to be faithful in reproduction (2 Timothy 2:2). As Paul was about to pass from the earth, he was concerned about the preservation of sound doctrine. So he instructed Timothy to pass it on to others who possessed two qualities: faithfulness and the ability to teach others. As Timothy was faithful in these things, Christian truth continued to flourish.

20. What are some strategies for passing on sound doctrine to faithful people?

The examples of faithfulness and the danger of unfaithfulness face us today. They both make the command to be faithful an urgent exhortation to us.

Making It Personal

21. Contemplate how God in Heaven will hold you safe in His arms until the Judgment Seat of Christ.

22. Commit yourself through prayer to faithfully obeying His Word until that day.

23. Memorize 2 Timothy 1:8.

Faithfulness Illustrated

Illustrations of faithfulness clearly demonstrate the exertion necessary to be faithful.

2 Timothy 2:3–13

"Thou therefore endure hardness, as a good soldier of Jesus Christ" (2 Timothy 2:3).

Imagine you have purchased the electric ride-on toy your child or grandchild has been dreaming of. After getting it home, you notice those fateful words, "Assembly Required," and the instructions are simply endless words. But all is not lost. Instructions with illustrations for each step are available online!

Getting Started

1. Would you use the verbal only instructions, or go online to get the illustrations?

2. Why would you make that choice?

3. How do illustrations help explain spiritual truths?

Searching the Scriptures

The Soldier

The first illustration of faithfulness is the soldier (2 Timothy 2:3). Paul challenged Timothy to endure hardness as a good soldier of Jesus Christ. The words "endure hardness" in the Greek contain the additional idea of "with." Timothy should endure hardness along with him (Paul).

4. Read 2 Timothy 2:3. What happens to a soldier if he gives up during hard times?

5. Read 2 Timothy 1:8. How can one endure hardness or partake of afflictions?

Living for God and being a faithful testimony of Jesus Christ brings hard times. The soldier of Christ must endure that hardness without fleeing in retreat, and God will provide the strength to do so.

6. Read 2 Timothy 2:4. What word in this verse speaks of a very arduous task?

7. Read 2 Timothy 2:4. What is the danger of becoming entangled as a soldier?

8. What are three things you would never lug around with you if you were on a battlefield?

Singleness of purpose is the main thrust of the illustration of faithfulness as demonstrated by a soldier. A Roman soldier did not get himself entangled in the affairs of this life, but gave himself wholeheartedly and undividedly to the one who chose him to be a soldier. Likewise, the soldiers of Christ are to be separate from love for the world, dedicated to the Lord, having a single purpose in life and that purpose, to please the Master. A focused purpose of pleasing God will increase our faithfulness.

The Athlete

9. Read 2 Timothy 2:5. What evidence of hard work do you see in this verse?

10. What would you think if you saw a person who was fifty pounds overweight standing at the starting line with a group of world-class sprinters?

The second illustration of faithfulness is that of an athlete. The words "strive for masteries" and then "strive" (v. 5) are both the same word in the Greek—*athleo,* from which we get our English word "athlete."

If a man competes as an athlete, he is not crowned unless he competes lawfully, according to the rules. The point of this illustration is found in the word "lawfully." Our faithful service to Christ must be done in accordance with the laws of Christ. Faithfulness is more than working for God; it is working for God within the boundaries of God's rules. Sometimes we speak of doing God's work in God's way.

11. What measures have sports taken recently to ensure that athletes are playing by the rules?

12. Read 2 Timothy 1:13. How would you connect 1:13 and 2:5?

The Farmer

13. Read 2 Timothy 2:6. What were some tough jobs that a farmer in Paul's day had to do?

The third illustration of faithfulness is that of a farmer. The key idea in verse 6 is the word "laboureth." It means to work to the point of exhaustion, pain, fatigue; to pour yourself into the toil until you are exhausted. One is reminded very pointedly that faithfulness involves hard work. It is keeping at it constantly as the farmer keeps tending his crops.

The three illustrations of soldier, athlete, and farmer show that faithfulness involves single-minded purpose, careful obedience, and hard work. What a challenge!

A sub-theme runs through these three illustrations: Faithfulness will be rewarded by God. Paul said that the soldier has the single-minded purpose of pleasing him who has chosen him. The Christian soldier wars so that he may hear the words of a pleased Commander, "Well done, thou good and faithful servant."

The athlete strives for the masteries that he might be crowned. The farmer who works hard is the first partaker of the fruits. He is the first one to enter into the rewards of his labor. The words of Jesus Christ at the end of the Beatitudes come to mind. Having just spoken about being persecuted and reviled and suffering, He said to rejoice and be exceedingly glad, for great reward awaits in Heaven (Matthew 5:12). If works are of the quality of gold, silver, and precious stone, they shall receive a reward from God (1 Corinthians 3:11–15). God will not forget a person's labor, but He will remember it and so reward it (Hebrews 6:10).

14. Read 2 Corinthians 5:10 and Revelation 22:12. Who will reward us for our faithful service, and when will we be rewarded?

Paul suffered trouble (2 Timothy 2:9). He was counted as an "evil-doer." Paul suffered for the gospel as someone who had committed a capital crime. In fact, he was facing death as he wrote. However, Paul endured all these troubles and did not let them turn him from being faithful to God (v. 10). He revealed two factors that aided him in being faithful.

First, Paul showed that the faithfulness of God motivated him to be faithful to God. He said to remember Jesus Christ as an encouragement (v. 8). Jesus was born of the seed of David in fulfillment of prophecy. He suffered to the point of death, but God vindicated Him and raised Him from the dead, again in fulfillment of prophecy. God is faithful to His Word.

15. Read 2 Timothy 2:8. If David were to appear with a message of God's faithfulness to his promises, what do you think would be part of his message?

These truths were according to the gospel that God had entrusted to Paul and for which Paul suffered (2 Timothy 2:9), so Timothy and believers today should take heart. Even though suffering occurs, God will be faithful to His Word to vindicate and reward the sufferer.

Paul sat in bonds as he wrote to Timothy, "But [strong contrast] the word of God [was] not bound" (v. 9). The Word of God cannot be bound. Throughout history people have tried to bind, ban, or destroy Scripture, but they never succeed. God's faithfulness in raising Christ and working through His Word incited Paul to faithfulness.

16. What often happens to the spread of God's Word in an area where people are trying to suppress it?

Paul endured all things for the sake of the elect, that they might obtain the salvation that is in Christ Jesus with eternal glory (2 Timothy

2:10). Paul taught the doctrine of divine election—that God had sovereignly chosen some, out of all who deserve Hell, to be saved. Far from being a hindrance for evangelism in Paul's life, election was a motivation to evangelism. And that is precisely what Paul said to Timothy. Paul viewed himself as God's messenger to take the gospel of salvation to all men so that those whom God had chosen would hear it and believe. He knew there would be results from his preaching. And since he was assured that people would be saved, he was willing to go through any kind of opposition so that those whom God had chosen would hear the message, believe it, and obtain salvation.

God ordains not only the ends, but the means as well. He has ordained that the chosen will be saved through the hearing of the gospel and the setting apart of the Holy Spirit (2 Thessalonians 2:13). Paul wanted to be part of God's program to bring His chosen to Himself, by letting them hear the gospel. The doctrine of election was a motivator to faithfulness for Paul.

17. Whose job is it to save people? Whose job is it to witness? Is either one less important than the other?

A well-known saying illustrates faithfulness. Verses 11–13 of 2 Timothy 2 may have been a hymn that the early Christians sang. If not a hymn, it must have been a saying so well-known that it was almost a cliché. The saying was one that could be counted upon because it remained accurate and true.

The saying is made up of four couplets, each one beginning with "if." The first two couplets refer to faithfulness, and the last two couplets refer to unfaithfulness.

The saying begins with the words, "If we be dead with him" (v. 11). Romans 6 says that Christians should reckon themselves dead to sin. If the believer has committed himself as a living sacrifice (Romans 12:1) so that he daily serves God as one who is dead to sin and alive to righteousness, then he will also live with Christ. If one is dead with Him in his service on this earth, he will live with Him in Heaven (2 Timothy 2:11).

The second couplet also refers to faithfulness. The word translated "suffer" (2 Timothy 2:12) is exactly the same word found in verse 10 and translated "endure." If one is faithful in suffering or enduring difficulty with Christ, he shall also reign with Him. Those who suffer with Him will be glorified with Him (Romans 8:17).

18. Evaluate this statement: Affliction for Christ is always bad, and we should pray that we never have to experience it.

Paul's last two couplets deal with unfaithfulness (2 Timothy 2:13). If we are unfaithful, God still abides faithful. He cannot deny Himself. There are some things God cannot do, not because He lacks the strength but because they would be self-contradictory. God will never contradict Himself. He always operates in harmony with the totality of His attributes. He cannot lie, because He is truth.

Some have interpreted this final couplet as a word of encouragement—that if we are unfaithful, He still abides faithful; so He will keep us and save us even if we are unfaithful. That interpretation seems to violate the flow of thought. The first two couplets spoke of faithfulness and the blessings that result. The last two speak about unfaithfulness and the judgment that results. Just as living with God and reigning with Him fit together as the two blessings of faithfulness, so His denying us must fit together with His abiding faithful.

19. How can God's faithfulness be a warning?

It is not possible for a genuine Christian to be lost. The Bible clearly teaches that true believers are saved forever. But the Bible also clearly teaches that there are many false professors. There are people who say they believe in Christ but who do not. The evidence of true faith is good works or godliness in living, as we saw in our study of Titus (Titus 3:8). John declared that we have assurance of salvation because we keep Christ's commandments (1 John 2:3, 4).

Paul warned, by use of this faithful saying, that if one makes denial of God the theme of his life, that person was never saved in the first place. God will deny him in faithfulness to His own warnings and judgments. He cannot do otherwise, for that would be to deny Himself.

This moves faithfulness out of the realm of the optional and puts it into the realm of the necessary. Paul did not pour out his heart here merely to say that faithfulness is a nice option and things would be much smoother if Christians practiced it. No, faithfulness is necessary as evidence of genuine conversion, as well as because God commands it. It is also necessary for the continuation of the faith, which was once for all delivered to the saints.

20. Read 1 Corinthians 4:1 and 2. What is a basic requirement for stewards?

Consider and Understand

Paul notified Timothy to consider what he was being told; the apostle's words were the very message of God (2 Timothy 2:7). Timothy was to consider the message and then the Lord would give him understanding. Here Paul alluded to meditation and illumination. Timothy would fully grasp the message of God as he meditated on it and God enlightened him to understand it.

21. Why will faithfulness to God never precede faithfulness to reading and meditating on God's Word?

It is difficult for Americans in the "rat race" to find time for meditation. And with miniaturized electronic devices of all kinds, the mind can be constantly bombarded from without. Christians today should carve

out time to consider God's Word, with prayer for the illuminating ministry of the Holy Spirit. The renewing of the mind through meditation and
illumination makes faithfulness to God a practical possibility.

Making It Personal

22. When was the last time you spent more than a few moments
considering God's Word?

If you are struggling with being faithful to God, the first thing to
consider is your time in His Word. We cannot expect to be faithful to
God without using His agent for change—the Bible.

23. Knowing the importance of faithfulness to God and the exertion
displayed by faithful people in this lesson, plan a specific way you can
give your all to faithfully serve Christ this week.

24. Memorize 2 Timothy 2:3.

Lesson 10

Faithfulness and Truth

The servant of God must interpret the Scriptures accurately and present the truth humbly.

2 Timothy 2:14–26

"Study to shew thyself approved unto God, a workman that needeth not to be ashamed, rightly dividing the word of truth" (2 Timothy 2:15).

Your five preschool-age grandchildren have all gathered to celebrate your birthday. As the cake is served, tears overflow Natalie's eyes and she begins to sob. You tenderly inquire about her distress and learn that she wanted the blue icing flower, not the green one.

Getting Started

1. How does Natalie's problem look from an adult's perspective?

2. Why does our interpretation or perspective of so many things change as we mature?

As believers, we are to mature in our understanding of the Word. We are to get better at handling it properly. We should eventually be able to help those who have fallen into doctrinal error. Paul wrote Timothy about dealing with those who were spreading false doctrines.

Searching the Scriptures

The Christian must not strive about words to no profit (2 Timothy 2:14), because they subvert the hearers. The word "subvert" is the word from which our English word "catastrophe" is derived. Striving about words to no profit causes spiritual catastrophe.

Christians should avoid striving about words to no profit. If a believer's mind is filled with the eternal issues of God, he is unlikely to get sidetracked into pointless controversy.

3. Read 1 Timothy 6:20 and 2 Timothy 2:16. What action was Timothy to take regarding profane and vain babblings?

4. What happens to ministry opportunities when we spend a lot of time reasoning with those who flatly deny the truth?

Shun Babblers

Verse 16 continues the thoughts of verse 14. God's follower must shun vain babblings, empty sounds, or comments that lack genuine merit, for they have nothing of holy character about them. Rather, they "increase unto more ungodliness." Babblers do not focus upon the Word of truth, where God Himself is revealed. Rather, they focus upon human ideas about God and explanations of life. As a result, their attitudes and behaviors become more and more ungodly. They themselves degenerate. Furthermore, what the babblers teach affects others in a detrimental way.

5. What would happen to a person's confidence in God's Word if he or she constantly heard from a fellow church member that it could not be trusted?

6. What are long-term consequences of a lack of confidence in God's Word?

Paul listed two people as examples of vain babblers, Hymenaeus and Philetus (v. 17). They had aimed to know the truth, but by getting involved in vain babblings, they veered away from it. Paul gave an example of their doctrine regarding the resurrection to illustrate how they had erred (v. 18).

7. Read 1 Corinthians 15:13 and 14. Explain the seriousness of denying bodily resurrection.

8. Babblers set themselves up as an authority over the Bible. What sin is at the root of such an action?

The Word of Truth

The man of God is to focus on the Word of truth (2 Timothy 2:15). The Word of truth for Timothy would have included the Old Testament and apostolic teaching. For us it would be the entire Bible.

9. Read John 17:17. How does Jesus describe God's Word?

10. What effect does God's Word have on those who belong to Christ?

Timothy was to be a workman in the things of God who rightly divided the Word of truth:

The workman of God is to interpret God's Word correctly, understanding its various doctrines and seeing one Scripture in the light of other Scriptures so that all fit together into one harmonious whole.

To rightly divide the Scriptures, Timothy needed to study (v. 15). The word "study" means "to have diligence" or "to give haste or to show eagerness." It has been interpreted by the translators as "study" because the context is one of handling the Word. We ought to study it with diligence, not just when it happens to be convenient. We ought to study it with haste, not rushing *through* it but rushing *to* it. We ought to do it with eagerness and willingness.

11. What are the benefits that come with handling God's Word properly?

The results of such diligent study of the Word are correct understanding of its meaning and God's approval. He will examine the workman's work and declare it acceptable, or the workman will be put to shame.

12. Read John 16:13. What ministry does the Holy Spirit have with regard to Christ's disciples and truth?

Foundation of God

In spite of the fact that there were some, even in the church, who were babblers, the foundation of God stands sure (2 Timothy 2:19).

"The foundation of God" seems to be a reference to the true people of God, that is, the church of God, which is His Body. The apostles were the foundation, with Jesus Christ the chief cornerstone (Ephesians 2:19–22). In the minds of the apostles the church had just begun to be built, and all that was really there was the foundational level. The church could be referred to easily as the foundation of God.

13. Read 1 Timothy 3:15. What is the church's relationship to the truth?

Two-sided Seal

The church stands sure, having a seal or inscription or identifying mark placed upon it by God (2 Timothy 2:19). The seal is a two-sided seal. First, the Lord knows them that are His (Numbers 16:5; John 10:14, 27). All in the visible church had professed faith in Christ. Some had their faith overthrown by babblers. But the church of God stands sure. From the Lord's viewpoint, God's people are safe, for He knows who they really are.

The second side of the seal warns, "Let everyone who names the name of Christ depart from iniquity" and presents the necessity of a godly lifestyle for Christians.

Some may become babblers, and others may have their faith overthrown by babblers, but an individual who belongs to God will be faithful.

To show what he meant by the command in verse 19, Paul used the example of a great household where there are vessels of gold and of silver, as well as of wood and of earth (clay). Some vessels are used for honorable purposes and some for ignoble purposes.

A believer must purge or cleanse himself from "these," but what are "these" (v. 21)? Some say they are the vessels of dishonor, which would be people. Others say that "these" refers to babblings and youthful lusts. Actually the two are similar, because the vessels of dishonor would be people who get involved in babbling and youthful lusts.

The principle of the illustration is separation. Christians are to be separate from ungodly practices and teachings and from so-called brothers who stubbornly continue in ungodly practices and teachings. Separation from such makes one a vessel fit for God's use.

14. Think of a vessel in your house that you would never drink out of because of how you have used it. How does that vessel help you understand the need to separate from ungodly practices and teachings?

15. Read 2 Timothy 2:22. What two things did Paul instruct Timothy to do?

In verse 22, Paul prescribed two actions for Timothy: fleeing and following. Fleeing with urgency is well-illustrated in Matthew 2:13 and 3:7. "Youthful lusts" would include a variety of desires that arise from the self-sufficiency that is characteristic of youthfulness. Timothy needed to flee from such desires, for they are self-centered, not God-centered.

Paul commanded Timothy to follow after faith, charity (or true love), and peace with a zeal comparable to that with which he was to flee from youthful lusts.

Controversy

Timothy was to avoid foolish and unlearned questions (2 Timothy 2:23; cf. v. 14), "profane and vain babblings" (v. 16), and words that eat like gangrene (v. 17). All these would be speculations outside the Word of God. Such speculations breed strife.

Verse 23 needs some explanation in the light of all Scripture. Is the Christian to avoid all controversy? No. Other passages teach that there is a proper place for pointing out error and defending the truth. Verses 24–26 state that the servant of the Lord must proclaim truth and correct those who teach error. Such action risks controversy, for those in error seldom submit easily to the truth.

16. Read Jude 3. What did Jude exhort his readers to do?

There is an important place for showing that a particular doctrine is unscriptural. But there also comes a time when the error has been so clearly exposed by Scripture that further explanations would be pointless. The Bible student argues his point and then rests his case at the appropriate time.

Also there are times when speculative teaching is proclaimed that does not find its base clearly in Scripture and that cannot clearly be refuted from Scripture. The Lord's children need to be careful about getting into controversy over speculative areas.

The message of verse 23 is not to avoid confronting foolish and unlearned questions but to avoid getting involved in useless arguments over them.

How can a believer be faithful to God when coming face-to-face with foolish and unlearned questions? First, the servant of the Lord must instruct opposers. The word "instructing" in verse 25 comes from the same root as the adjective "unlearned" in verse 23. Opposers raise uninstructed questions. God's servant gives the Biblical instruction that will properly deal with those questions. God's servant stands up to the babbler and points out where his babblings are wrong according to the Word of God, which the servant has rightly divided.

17. Read Hebrews 12:10. "Chastened" translates the same Greek word as "instructing" in 2 Timothy 2:25. What is God's purpose in chastening/instructing you, and how does that relate to 2 Timothy 2:25?

Babblers are described as those who put themselves in opposition. Some translations render the expression in verse 25 "oppose themselves"; and others render it "oppose him," that is, the servant. Both are true, for whenever a person wrests Scriptures or rejects the truth, he does it to the detriment of his own soul.

Confronting Babblers

The Lord's servant must not get involved in producing strife but must be gentle to all, able to teach, patient (v. 24), and meek (v. 25). As he clearly and accurately presents the truth and is opposed, he must not become personally insulted. It is not his truth or honor that is at stake, but God's. He must be sure that what he says is God's truth, and he should be as patient as Christ, Who did not revile those who reviled Him but even sought their forgiveness by the Father. The servant realizes that only by God's grace has he come to understand and value God's truth, so he instructs the babbler with an attitude of meekness. The servant does not ignore babblers. He stands up to them and confronts their babblings.

18. Read Galatians 6:1. What will happen if someone deals with a person in error but does it without a sense of his or her own weaknesses?

The ultimate purpose in instructing opposers is not to embarrass them, nor even to merely prove them wrong, though that may be a step. The goal is that they might repent and come to know the truth (v. 26). It is the love of the truth of God that drives God's servant to study and defend the Bible. And God's servant desires that the babbler might come to view the truth with the same love.

19. Read 2 Thessalonians 2:10. What does this verse imply that all the saved have received?

Learning spiritual truth involves more than mere human teaching. The unsaved person does not understand spiritual things (1 Corinthians 2:14). The Holy Spirit must teach an individual, so the babbler will acknowledge the truth only if God gives him repentance. Paul did not know what would happen to these babblers, whether they would continue in their vanity or if God would give them repentance (2 Timothy 2:25). So the Lord's servant Timothy needed to instruct them with gentleness, meekness, and patience and trust God to work as He would.

Captive by Satan

The devil is behind vain babblings, for he has intoxicated and snared people's minds with the drunkenness of godless philosophy (v. 26). The babblers have been taken captive by Satan at his will, though they would probably consider themselves free from the narrow constraints of God's Word .

20. Evaluate this statement: The more a person fights to be free of God's Word, the more ensnared he or she becomes.

To be faithful to God in the area of controversy is to stand up for the truth, being able to present it clearly to others. It is to instruct others; having the right attitudes and for the right purpose. And it is to do all this with a sense of dependence upon God, realizing that ultimately He is the One Who must give repentance.

Making It Personal

21. What can you do to better divide the truth of God's Word? About what doctrines are you unsure? Consider securing a good basic doctrinal book to help form a basis for understanding and rightly using God's Word. Ask your pastor for his recommendations.

22. Select someone with whom you believe you should share some truth of God's Word. Arrange a time this week to do so, and pray that God will use the time to profit both of you.

23. Memorize 2 Timothy 2:15.

Faithfulness and Apostasy

*We deal with opposition and false teaching
by faithfully continuing in the inspired
Scripture, which provides the mind
of God for every area of life.*

2 Timothy 3

**"But continue thou in the things which thou
hast learned and hast been assured of, knowing
of whom thou hast learned them" (2 Timothy
3:14).**

Afather took his son to a baseball card show when he
was a young boy. The father bought a ball and his son
got some autographs. One signer made the little boy's heart sink when
he "ruined" the ball by "scribbling" on it—his penmanship was definitely
subpar. In disgust the little boy stored the ball away. It turned up about
twenty years later, and the young man was shocked to read the scribbled
autograph—Cy Young.

Getting Started

1. How could the young man's experience with the autographed
baseball parallel the experience many of us have had with God's Word?

2. When was the last time you read a familiar passage and gained a fresh insight?

Today's study is about the powerful, transforming nature of God's Word.

Searching the Scriptures

3. Read 2 Timothy 3:1. What comes to your mind when you think of perilous times coming in the last days?

The word for "times" could be translated "seasons." The Greek language has several words for time, and this word refers to time with a view toward its quality. We may talk about good times, happy times, or sad times; in so doing we describe their nature or quality. In the last days there will be seasons that are perilous. They will be dangerous to the Christian because of opposition, and as a result they will be difficult to endure.

Timothy was living in the last days, and he was facing one of the perilous seasons. Paul described the kind of people who would make the seasons perilous and then told Timothy specifically to turn away from such people.

Character and Deeds of Reprobates

The times will be perilous "for" or because a certain type of person will create problems. Paul named nineteen character qualities of these reprobates in verses 2–5 so that Christians might be able to identify such people.

The first quality is "lovers of their own selves." The word "love" is phileo, or affection, rather than agape, or caring concern. They have affection for themselves, yet at the same time they lack affection for good and for God (vv. 3, 4).

Next, they are "covetous." Literally, this word means to be a lover of silver.

4. Read 1 Timothy 6:10. What is the root of all sorts of evil?

The third quality characterizes them as boasters. They brag and elevate themselves to great heights. This behavior is closely related to the fourth quality, pride. Reprobates like to appear superior to others, so they boast in an attempt to lift themselves to a higher level than those around them.

5. Read James 4:6. What is God's response to proud people?

Lack of Respect for God

"Blasphemers," speaks of those who lack respect for God and say evil things about Him. Disobedience to parents shows that they lack respect for their earthly fathers, as well as for the Heavenly Father. They generally do not submit to authority.

They are "unthankful." This indicates a lack of conscious dependence upon God. Thankfulness comes easily when someone is aware of his total dependence upon God for every good gift.

They are "unholy." The description is not so much of a life of sinful practices (though they do live in sin) but of a lack of respect for the sacred. In addition to lacking respect for God, gratitude toward God, and a sense of dependence upon God, they lack respect for anything that is associated with God or is holy.

6. List some ways that "unholy" people make times perilous for believers.

Reprobates are without the affection that would be normal by nature (2 Timothy 3:3). Affection toward other family members is strangely missing. The description "trucebreakers" means they are unbound by covenants. They feel no obligation to keep a promise, whether it is spoken or written. They lack appreciation for the sanctity of promises.

"False accusers" translates the word *diabolos,* from which we get "devil," the accuser of the brethren. Reprobates do not hesitate to point fingers at others and place blame on others, even without assurance that the charges are true.

"Incontinent" probably applies to self-control. Since unbelievers in the last days lack self-control, they appear to be fierce, untamed, or savage. Their lack of self-control becomes so extensive that they could be compared to wild beasts. Whenever their emotions are stirred, they just act out the way they feel.

"Despisers of those that are good" reminds us of Romans 1:32, which says that evil people not only commit things that are worthy of death but have pleasure in others who do such things. They enjoy evil people and despise good. The expression Paul used in 2 Timothy 3:3 could include good things, good beliefs, and good events as well good people.

7. Read Titus 1:8. How does the qualification of a pastor contrast with the character of these people?

Traitors

"Traitors" are willing to hurt someone else for their own gain (2 Timothy 3:4). They would betray a friend, an acquaintance, and certainly a Christian. The word "stubborn" would appropriately convey "heady" in contemporary speech. The minds of these people without God have been made up, and they do not want to be bothered with the facts of God's truth.

We use the word "high-minded" in a positive sense to mean someone who has noble and worthy thoughts. The idea in verse 4 is quite different. It describes those whose heads are in a cloud. They think they know everything, but they are really in a fog and do not see reality clearly.

"Lovers of pleasures more than lovers of God" are those who choose pleasure rather than God and His will. The hedonism of our day teaches people to do whatever they want to do, not what they ought to do.

8. What are some evidences that our society is becoming more and more a society of lovers of pleasure more than lovers of God?

Denying the Power

The final quality is "having a form of godliness, but denying the power thereof." These people are religious and profess to be following God.

Two additional character qualities of these reprobates are given in verse 8. First, they were people of corrupt minds. Sin affects thinking so that a person does not think the way God thinks. The people of whom Paul spoke had minds that were spoiled or depraved.

9. Read Ephesians 4:22 and 23. What remedy does God provide for the depravity of our minds?

Second, they were reprobate concerning the faith. "The faith" means the truth, or the faith once for all delivered to the saints. These people were unapproved or disapproved by God with regard to doctrine because they departed from the truth.

The deeds of some of these people, certain ones "of this sort," fall into two categories. First, they "creep into houses" and "lead captive" those who live there (2 Timothy 3:6): "creep" because they presented themselves as servants of God, but were not; "lead captive," because, once inside, they made the dwellers captive to false teaching and ultimately to Satan (cf. 2 Timothy 2:25, 26). These false teachers directed their ministry toward women.

Pity should swell in our hearts as we read the description of these captivated women. Paul summarized their spiritual condition in three statements. First, they were silly (3:6). Second, the women are laden with sins. They were burdened with a conscious weight of sins and captive to various desires of the flesh (v. 6). Third, they were ever learning and never able to come to the truth (v. 7).

10. Read 2 Timothy 3:6 and 7. How can a church ensure that it is not allowing reprobates into teaching positions?

In addition to creeping into houses and leading unwise women astray, these people also resisted the truth (v. 8). They practiced and promoted error.

At this point Timothy received a word of encouragement: such people would proceed no further, for their folly would be manifest unto all men as Jannes's and Jambres's was also (vv. 8, 9).

The question arises, they shall proceed no further than what? No further than they already had? That answer would be contradicted by 2 Timothy 3:13. The word "wax" is the same word translated "increase" in 2:16 and "proceed" in 3:9. Evil people and seducers proceed to become worse and worse. The best answer would be that they should proceed no further than God permits. This understanding accords with the overall teaching of the Bible.

11. Read Job 1:10. What had God done to limit how far even Satan could go?

Timothy's Comprehension

Paul's faithfulness was "fully known" to Timothy (2 Timothy 3:10). The little word "my" in verse 10 belongs with each of the things mentioned in verses 10 and 11. Paul set himself before Timothy as an example. Paul had been through perilous times, and Timothy knew it. But Timothy also knew that Paul had endured and that God had delivered Paul. Timothy comprehended a shining example of faithfulness.

12. How have you benefited in your Christian walk through the examples of others?

Paul then expressed a staggering promise—Timothy and those faithful to God through the ages could expect the same kind of treatment that Paul had received. That is, persecution (v. 12)!

Timothy's Continuance

Paul spent the remainder of chapter 3 speaking of the Word of God, the source of sound doctrine.

13. Read 2 Timothy 3:15. What are the Scriptures able to do?

The Scriptures "are able" to make one wise unto salvation (v. 15). This is an enduring quality of the Word that was true in Timothy's day, and it continues to be true today. Salvation is through faith, and faith comes by hearing the Word of God.

Verse 16 speaks of the source of the Scriptures. All Scripture is "given by inspiration of God," which is a translation of just one word in the Greek. It means "God-breathed." When someone speaks, he breathes out. The Scriptures are God's out-breathings; they are God's Word.

14. What better reason is there to stay faithful to God's Word than the fact that they are inspired?

Notice that all the writings were inspired, not just the religious statements or merely certain books or passages. The text says "all scripture."

Some prefer the translation "every Scripture," but whichever way you take it, you come to the same inescapable conclusion that the whole Bible and each and every one of its parts is God-breathed.

How could fallible people who make many mistakes write down a message that was God-breathed and without error?

15. Read 2 Peter 1:21. What did the Holy Spirit do to ensure that God's Word was recorded as God intended it to be?

This gives a glimpse into the method God used to ensure accuracy. The men were "moved" by the Holy Spirit. That does not mean they were motivated or encouraged. The word "move" means to carry along or to bear as a stream would bear a leaf. As the stream changes speed or direction, the leaf does likewise. Similarly, the Holy Spirit controlled the writers, and what they wrote was free from their fallibility.

Verses 16 and 17 speak of service and the Scripture. The Word of God is profitable for both belief and behavior. A Christian believes certain things and acts in certain ways; that is, when one receives Christ his mind is illuminated to accept the doctrines of the Word, and his behavior is altered to fit the commandments of the Word. This does not happen in an instant in the total sense, but the direction of the mind and behavior is reversed, and growth begins to take place.

The Word of God is profitable for doctrine, teaching us what we should believe. It is profitable for reproof, pointing out what is wrong in both our beliefs and behaviors. It is profitable for correction, showing what right thing should be substituted for the wrong. And it is profitable for training in righteous living, which may summarize the first three points.

16. Read 2 Timothy 3:16. How have you seen the reality of the transforming nature of God's Word in your life?

The goal of the profitableness of Scripture is that the man of God may be complete, equipped, fitted out just right. The word translated "thoroughly furnished" is from the same root as "perfect." The Bible completely equips the believer to do everything that God considers good and wants done. The Bible comes from God, shows us how to get to God, and makes us useful in His service. Therefore, proclaim the Word!

17. Given the transforming nature of God's Word, what can a church do to ensure that God's Word is at the center of its ministry?

Making It Personal

Some people are more faithful to their favorite TV program, newspaper, or recipe book than they are to God's Word. That is a shame when you think of the transforming power of God's Word.

Meditate on the amazing fact that God breathed the very words of Scripture. Consider that Scripture is able to make one wise unto salvation and perfectly outfit you to do everything God wants.

18. Will you covenant with God to remain true to His incredible Word?

19. Memorize 2 Timothy 3:14.

Faithfulness in Ministry

There are reasons for and specific activities that define faithful ministry.

2 Timothy 4:1–8

"I have fought a good fight, I have finished my course, I have kept the faith: Henceforth there is laid up for me a crown of righteousness, which the Lord, the righteous judge, shall give me at that day: and not to me only, but unto all them also that love his appearing" (2 Timothy 4:7, 8).

Members in each chapter of Weight Watchers meet in a church or an office once a week to have their weight watched. Sounds silly, but the fact that someone else is seeing a member's weight on the scale is the reason Weight Watchers is so successful. Weekly accountability motivates people to drop the pounds. Of course, the motivation to lose weight works only if you show up consistently at the meetings. People who stop going stop losing weight.

Getting Started

1. What is the power of accountability?

2. What experience do you have with accountability?

Every believer is accountable to Christ, our Judge. Paul developed
that truth in his message to Timothy.

Searching the Scriptures

Solemn Responsibility

Paul gave Timothy a charge, the solemn responsibility to be faithful
(2 Timothy 4:1). The Father and the Son served as witnesses of Timothy's charge. Timothy would be serving "before" (that is, "in the sight
of") Deity. Furthermore, God "shall" judge. The word "shall" is not merely a future tense but a word that means "about to." That stresses two
ideas. First the judging is certain; there is to be no possibility of escap-
ing it. Second, the judging is imminent. God is about to judge, so there
must be no delay in obeying the charge. Timothy's solemn responsibility rested upon his accountability to God.

3. Read 2 Timothy 4:1. Why do we tend to see other people as our
judges when we minister?

When the Lord judges, those who are living at His return and those
who have already died will all be judged (v. 1). So whether Christ
should come before or after Timothy's death, He would still be Timothy's Judge and would evaluate how Timothy fulfilled his charge. What
a powerful incentive to faithfulness.

The phrase "at his appearing and his kingdom" would seem to focus upon time, but the idea becomes clearer if we render the text "by
his appearing and by his kingdom." Timothy faced perilous times, as we
do today. But there will come a day when perilous times cease and the
glorious kingdom of God fills the earth. Therefore, Timothy was not to
be afraid in the face of opposition. God is coming again to overthrow
all opposition and make this world His kingdom.

These truths are solid reasons to be faithful to this charge.

4. How often do you think about standing before Christ, your Judge?

5. How should it affect your service for the Lord?

The Reward that Awaits

Timothy's charge to faithfulness was also based upon the reward that awaits the faithful servant.

6. Read 2 Timothy 4:6–8. What three periods does Paul address?

Paul said he was ready to be offered, to have his life poured out like a drink offering to the Lord. (See Numbers 15:5, 7, and 10.) When Paul was beheaded, he poured himself out as a drink offering to God.

The time of his departure was at hand (2 Timothy 4:6). He saw his death as being present and ready to happen. His word for "departure" was commonly used of death.

7. Read Philippians 1:23. Where did Paul know he would be after departing this life, and how did he evaluate that location?

Paul looked back over his life and described it under three figures. First of all, he had fought a good fight (2 Timothy 4:7). This figure could refer to just about any athletic event, but perhaps wrestling was the specific sport on his mind. Second, he had finished the course. This figure pictures the runner who has given his fullest effort and has reached the tape at last. Third, he had kept the faith. This figure brings to mind the soldier who has faithfully guarded something committed to his care.

8. What, if anything, is better than coming to the end of your life knowing that you did what God wanted you to do?

Since Paul had been faithful, a crown of righteousness awaited him (v. 8). Athletic winners in Paul's day received a leafy garland as a crown for their victories. It had little value in itself but was held in high esteem because of the honor it signified. In Heaven a token of great honor was reserved for Paul by God Himself.

9. Read 1 John 3:2 and 3. What does everyone who has the hope of seeing and being like Christ when He comes do?

All those who love Christ's appearing can receive a crown because they who have that hope live righteously (2 Timothy 4:8). The potential of reward in Heaven is another solid reason to be faithful to this charge.

10. What evidence in your life suggests that you are consciously looking forward to Heaven?

A third basis for Paul's charge to Timothy is introduced in verses 3 and 4 by the word "for." A difficult time will come. It will be a time when many will not endure sound doctrine. Opposition arises from those who cannot endure to sit under the authority of sound doctrine.

11. Read 1 Corinthians 1:18. What two groups are named, and how do those two view the message of Christ's cross differently?

Those who cannot endure sound doctrine react by getting out from under the preaching of it. We might expect they would stop attending services, but human beings are incurably religious. If a person will not worship the true God in the proper way, he will worship otherwise. Those who reject God's way find teachers who do not teach sound doctrine.

12. What does your fleshly self want to do when you hear a message or a Sunday School lesson that convicts you of sin?

Itching Ears

These people had ear trouble (2 Timothy 4:3). Their ears itched to hear self-complimentary things. The teachers taught what the listeners wanted to hear.

Notice three contrasts between the first and last parts of verse 4, which give the results of ear-scratching preaching. First, they turned away from the truth and unto fables. Fables are beliefs that are not in accord with truth.

A second contrast has to do with actively turning and passively being turned. The people who will not endure sound doctrine *turn themselves away* from the truth. In the end they find themselves *being turned* by someone else. They do not intend to believe fables when they set out. But once they forsake the truth, they have no objective standard by which to judge a message. The teachers they choose tell them what they want to hear and eventually lead them to believe fables.

A third contrast is found in the two words for "turn." In the first half of verse 4 the verb and its prefix have the idea of "turn away from." In the last half of the verse the verb and its prefix convey the idea of turning out of the proper place. The resisters of sound doctrine turn themselves away from the truth, and then they are turned out of the proper place. They refuse to listen to sound doctrines, and their faith is dislocated and made to rest on fables.

13. Have you known someone who turned from the truth and ended up being turned aside to false doctrine? What characterized their lives after they turned from the truth?

Preach the Word

Five behaviors characterize faithfulness in ministry (2 Timothy 4:2): preaching, being instant, reproving, rebuking, and exhorting. To preach the Word is to proclaim the Word with authority. When speaking for God, only the Word of God can be proclaimed with authority, for it alone has come from God.

14. What happens to the power of God's Word when the person preaching it almost apologizes for the message as if the people don't have to take it seriously?

The word "instant" (v. 2) means "be present and ready." Timothy was to be present and ready to preach the Word and to do any type of ministry for which God had equipped him. Timothy was to minister when he was well-received and things seemed to be going well ("in season"). And he was to minister when there was opposition and results seemed meager ("out of season").

When believers practice forbidden things, they need the reproof of the Word through faithful ministers. So Timothy was to "reprove." "Rebuke," on the other hand, is stronger than "reprove" and is probably directed toward those who are not convicted by reproof.

15. Evaluate this statement: A pastor should rebuke people only if he feels comfortable doing it.

Exhort

The word "exhort" is the verb form of the Greek word *paraclete,* or comforter. The servant of the Lord is to comfort, strengthen, or encourage others in doing right.

Notice that the ministries of reproof, rebuke, and exhortation were to be done in a particular manner—with all long-suffering and doctrine. The Lord's servant needs long-suffering and patience if he is to be faithful in reproving and rebuking. Also, some people readily agree that their behavior is wrong and to what they should do, but they seem to have difficulty accomplishing what they agree to do. The Lord's servant must be long-suffering in strengthening them and moving them along.

16. Read Colossians 1:11. What enables us to exercise such long-suffering?

These ministries demand not only long-suffering but doctrine. As we have seen, the Scripture is profitable for doctrine. As the servant of the Lord shows another what is wrong, he must present what the Bible says is wrong, and not just his opinion of the problem. And as he shows others what is right, that, too, must be what the Bible says is right. Finally, as he gives encouragement, he should give Biblical encouragement concerning the greatness of our God and His ever-abiding presence to help.

Watch

Timothy was to watch in all things (2 Timothy 4:5). He was to be watchful in the areas of doctrine, behavior, life, and faith, watching both himself and others. The word "watch" in verse 5 means to be sober, either literally or metaphorically. One can be sober or not drunk with wine, and one can be sober-minded, alert, and attentive. Certainly both levels are appropriate for the servant of the Lord.

17. What can a pastor do to be aware of what is going on in the lives of the church members?

Timothy was also to endure afflictions, do the work of an evangelist, and make full use proof of his ministry. An evangelist was a preacher of the gospel. He was much like a modern-day missionary in going to people who did not know the gospel to preach to them, build them up in the Lord, and establish them as a local church.

Timothy, for the time, was limited geographically, but he was urged to remember the unsaved. He must not get so immersed in caring for the flock and fighting the reprobates that he forgot the unsaved.

Finish the Course

Timothy was to fulfill his ministry (2 Timothy 4:5; cf. Acts 12:25). He was not to forsake it, but to faithfully carry it to completion. He was to finish his course, even as Paul had finished his. Timothy was to be faithful to the very end.

Just a word about Timothy's "ministry." The word itself means "service." It is related to the word from which we derive "deacon" or "servant." In twenty-first century America the word "ministry" is often attached to the functions of ordained men and considered a profession. The ministry, in the sense of pastoral service, is a noble place of service. But it is still service, and the minister is basically a servant of the Lord.

18. Read John 12:26. Who can be a servant of the Lord?

Every believer is a minister/servant of Christ. The challenge to be faithful in ministry to the very end is a challenge to every Christian.

Making It Personal

19. Review the behaviors of ministry and select one you believe God would have you practice this week. Put on your calendar time to pray about it and to practice it. Since it will most likely involve other people, make arrangements with them as soon as possible.

20. Memorize 2 Timothy 4:7 and 8.

Faithfulness and Paul's Companions

Companionship in ministry is vital, and the Lord's companionship is essential.

2 Timothy 4:9–22

"And the Lord shall deliver me from every evil work, and will preserve me unto his heavenly kingdom: to whom be glory for ever and ever. Amen" (2 Timothy 4:18).

You are camping in a remote area known for wild animals. During the late fall night, a fierce thunderstorm rips your tent and drenches everything. You have no choice but to hike more than a mile through the woods to your vehicle. Which of the following would be most reassuring as you travel: dry clothes, your favorite cookies, someone to go with you, or an MP3 player?

Getting Started

1. How does being alone impact our feelings in a fearful situation?

2. What value would a companion be during your trek?

Paul closed his letter to Timothy with a look at companions in ministry.

Searching the Scriptures

The three New Testament letters we have studied present three successive themes. Philemon teaches forgiveness, Titus shows godliness, and 2 Timothy demonstrates faithfulness.

Companions Who Strayed

One companion who strayed was Demas. He had been with Paul during Paul's first Roman imprisonment (Colossians 4:14; Philemon 24). But by the time Paul wrote 2 Timothy, Demas had forsaken Paul. The word Paul used to speak of the forsaking gave the idea of leaving a person in a difficult situation. Demas not only left Paul, but he left him at a time when Paul really needed him (2 Timothy 4:10).

Demas left Paul because he loved "this present world." He loved the world just as the Christian is supposed to love the appearing of Christ (same word is used for love in 4:10 and 4:8).

3. Read 1 John 2:15. Loving the world (system) is evidence of what grave problem?

Imagine yourself on trial for a capital crime. The death penalty awaits if you are found guilty. You have no lawyer and no one willing to be a witness on your behalf. That's where Paul stood (2 Timothy 4:16). No man stood as a witness, and no man stood as an advocate or attorney with Paul. There were Christians in Rome at the time, but when the trial began, they were nowhere to be found. Luke must have arrived later, for he was present as Paul wrote (v. 11). Paul sought God's forgiveness for those who had deserted him, even as Christ asked forgiveness for His crucifiers and as Stephen did for those who stoned him.

4. Read 2 Timothy 4:16. What did Paul demonstrate about the value he placed on companions in ministry by forgiving those who had deserted him?

Companions Who Stayed

In verse 10, Paul mentioned two companions who stayed with him: Crescens and Titus. Crescens had been with Paul earlier, but by the time Paul was writing to Timothy, Crescens had departed to Galatia, which was some distance east of Ephesus, where Timothy was serving at that time. You will recall that Titus was in Crete. Sometime between his meeting with Paul at Nicopolis (Titus 3:12) and Paul's trial, Titus had gone to Dalmatia. There is no reason to believe that Crescens and Titus had loved the present world and deserted Paul (2 Timothy 4:10). More likely, they had left Paul for further ministries in Galatia and Dalmatia, probably at Paul's direction. So Crescens and Titus continued to be faithful companions of Paul, even though they were not present with him at this time.

5. Read 1 Corinthians 5:3. What companionship, mentioned in principle in this verse, could Paul have enjoyed with Crescens and Titus?

The only worker in the gospel still with Paul as he wrote was Luke, the doctor (2 Timothy 4:11). Luke was with Paul rather consistently (though not constantly) from the middle of the second missionary journey, through the third, the imprisonment in Caesarea, the trip to Rome and the first imprisonment, and finally, the second imprisonment. It is interesting that the Gentile doctor, Luke, would be the only one with Paul during his final days.

Paul may have sent Tychicus (v. 12) to be Timothy's replacement so that Timothy could visit Paul (vv. 9, 21). He may have been the one who carried this very epistle from Paul to Timothy. So, by the time Timothy would read the letter, Tychicus would have already been sent and Paul's past tense ("I have sent") would be appropriate.

6. Read Colossians 4:7. What glowing description did Paul make of his companion Tychicus?

Paul had sent Timothy and a believer named Erastus together into Macedonia during the third missionary journey (Acts 19:22). Timothy would have been interested in knowing what had become of this companion. So Paul told him that Erastus had stayed at Corinth (2 Timothy 4:20).

Paul also mentioned Trophimus, who had been with Paul in Jerusalem after the third missionary trip and was indirectly the cause of the uproar that led to Paul's arrest (Acts 21:26–31). Since Paul had a Gentile with him in Jerusalem, some Jews thought (incorrectly) that Paul had taken a Gentile into the temple. On the basis of that false assumption, the Jews rioted.

Since Trophimus had been a companion of the Christians at Ephesus (Acts 21:29), Paul told Timothy and the people there what had become of him (2 Timothy 4:20). Paul had left him sick at Miletus ("Miletum").

7. What does Paul's list of faithful ministers teach you about the need for companions in ministry?

My Son Timothy

Paul gave Timothy four instructions and a blessing as he came to the end of the letter.

First, Paul requested that Timothy leave his post in Ephesus and come to be with him in Rome (2 Timothy 4:21). Timothy was to be diligent in his efforts to make the visit, giving it high priority and intense concentration.

8. Read 2 Timothy 4:9. What are some possible reasons why Paul desired Timothy's visit?

Paul was in a difficult situation and desired human companionship. He was trusting in the Lord, but he also desired the presence of a faithful friend. All his other friends, except for Luke, had either been sent on ministry trips or had deserted.

Paul also wanted Timothy to come before winter set in. First of all, travel in the winter was dangerous, as Paul knew by experience (Acts 27). Secondly, Paul needed his coat before the winter cold invaded his cell.

Cloak and Books

Paul asked that Timothy bring a cloak (2 Timothy 4:13). The cloak was a heavy coat that would provide some warmth in the cold jail cell. Paul had left it at Troas with Carpus during his travels between the two imprisonments.

9. Read 2 Timothy 4:13. Why would Paul want Scriptures while he was alone is prison?

Paul requested that Timothy bring the books and the parchments. The books were writings on papyrus. The parchments were writings on animal skins. The parchments likely contained the Old Testament Scriptures, and Paul especially wanted those. It is noteworthy that Paul still wanted to study, especially the Scripture, even as death was approaching. He practiced what he preached (2:15). What a challenge to us! Many of us seldom read a book or dig into the Word. Paul was a student of the Word up to the day of his execution.

Send Mark

Paul also requested Timothy to bring John Mark with him. John Mark had left Paul during the first missionary journey (Acts 13:5, 13). When Paul and Barnabas were ready to begin the second journey, a dispute arose between them over John Mark (Acts 15:36–41). Paul would not let John Mark go because of his previous desertion.

But by the time of Paul's first imprisonment, Mark had been restored to fellowship with Paul (Colossians 4:10; Philemon 24). And as Paul was imprisoned the second time, he desired Mark's presence.

10. Read 2 Timothy 4:11. How did Paul describe Mark?

Paul also gave Timothy a warning: beware of a man named Alexander, the coppersmith (vv. 14, 15). The word "coppersmith" could mean a worker in copper or any metal. Perhaps this man made silver idols of Diana. He may have been one of the workers who rioted over Paul's influence in Ephesus during the third missionary trip (Acts 19:23ff.)

Alexander did Paul much evil. Paul desired the Lord to reward him according to his works (2 Timothy 4:14). This may be a simple statement of fact that the Lord would reward him that way. Or it may have been Paul's desire that the Lord would reward him in such a manner. If this man did oppose God and His gospel, then God, the righteous Judge, would be right in bringing a judgment against him. And Paul could seek that judgment, not out of personal revenge, but out of a sincere desire for God's honor. Remember Paul's totally different attitude toward those who forsook him personally but did not fight against the work of the Lord (v. 16).

Paul suspected that Alexander would continue to oppose the truth of God as Timothy and other Christians proclaimed it in Ephesus. Therefore, Timothy was to guard himself against Alexander.

11. Read 2 Timothy 4:15. What benefit of companionships did Paul's warning about Alexander demonstrate?

Timothy was also to give Paul's greetings to Priscilla and Aquila (v. 18). This couple had fled from Rome because of persecution against the Jews. They had been with Paul in several places (Acts 18:2, 18). Now they were in Ephesus, serving the Lord with Timothy.

Onesiphorus, a very faithful companion of Paul's and resident of Ephesus, received Paul's greetings along with his household.

12. Read 2 Timothy 4:22. What companionship did Paul request for Timothy?

Paul desired God's greatest blessings to rest upon Timothy (v. 22). The word "spirit" is used very similarly to the word "soul" in the Bible, and yet there seems to be the distinction that the spirit is our nonmaterial part related to God. Paul desired the favorable presence of Christ and His grace to be consciously present with Timothy.

The Lord

As Paul neared the conclusion of his letter with its focus on faithfulness, he had no more fitting end than to turn Timothy's attention to the faithful One, God Himself. Paul proclaimed the great faithfulness of God, Who alone was faithful to Paul in his greatest hour of need.

13. Read 2 Timothy 4:17. How important was the Lord to Paul while Paul stood trial?

When Paul had his trial, God stood with him (v. 17). No human being was present to support him, but God was faithful to His promise never to leave (Hebrews 13:5). Paul had been faithfully carrying out the Great Commission, and Jesus never left him (Matthew 28:19, 20). Paul sensed the Lord standing by his side as he endured the anguish of his trial, and ministering to him.

14. Read John 19:26. Who stood by Jesus Christ at His darkest hour?

God strengthened Paul as he stood before the tribunal (2 Timothy 4:17). He strengthened Paul so that his preaching might be fully known to the Gentiles. Paul's trial would have been a sensational hearing. Roman governmental dignitaries other than the required legal officials may have packed the courtroom. Paul had no lawyer, and so he spoke in his own behalf. Since he was on trial for preaching the gospel, it would be relevant for his defense to have included a clear presentation of the gospel.

124 FROM FORGIVEN TO FAITHFULNESS

15. Read Philippians 4:12 and 13. What had Paul learned earlier in his ministry that he found true at this crucial time in his life?

This courtroom scene could easily have been viewed as an "out of season" time for preaching. Paul could have tried to rationalize his way out of doing it. But he saw the situation as a choice time to preach Christ, and the Lord strengthened him to do so.

God delivered him out of the lion's mouth. The lion may have meant Caesar, king of the empire. It may have meant Satan (1 Peter 5:8). Paul may have intended it to convey death, as in Psalm 22:21. All three combine nicely, for Satan was the unseen force working through Caesar to bring Paul to death. But God delivered him at that point.

God would deliver Paul from every evil work. Paul was going to die soon (2 Timothy 4:6), so he did not mean God would keep him from death. The preservation would extend even through death and into Heaven. God would keep Paul from recanting and becoming unfaithful, even through execution. And God would keep Paul safe from the forces of evil who would like to snatch him out of God's hands and thwart God's plan for his life. And so Paul ended with a doxology to God (v. 18). God was faithful to Paul, and Paul would be faithful to his Lord all the way to Heaven, for God was able to keep that which Paul had committed to Him until that day.

16. What has your companionship with the Lord done for you over the years?

Making It Personal

17. To whom could you provide the blessing of Christian companionship this week? Could you assist that person in their ministry for Christ or request their assistance with your ministry? Could you share

with that person a testimony of God's faithfulness to you?

18. Contact an old friend that you haven't talked to in a while. Write him or her a note of thanks for companionship through the years.

19. Memorize 2 Timothy 4:18.